GOVERNING CHURCHES

CHURCHES

&
ANTIOCH APOSTLES

DISCOVERING THE
NEW APOSTOLIC REFORMATION!

by
Jonas Clark

Spirit of Life Ministries
Hallandale, Florida

Governing Churches

Unless otherwise indicated, all Scripture quotations are taken from the *King James Version* of the Bible.

Governing Churches & Antioch Apostles
ISBN 1-886885-07-9
First Edition

Published by Spirit of Life Publishing

ABOUT
THE AUTHOR

Jonas Clark is a refreshing voice of a champion in the contemporary church today. He is the founding apostle of Spirit of Life Ministries in Hallandale, Florida and the pioneer of The Global Cause Network, a fellowship of churches around the world of like precious faith. Fortitude and God's grace have also taken the ministry international into over 23 nations, carrying a message of divine impact and reform for this generation. The anointing on his life is both strong and bold. As a revivalist, his desire is to see the nations of the world impacted by the power of God. As an apostolic ministry gift and author, he is refreshing, intense, exciting, bold, and sold out to Jesus. Jonas has written several books with an apostolic and prophetic voice that is catching the attention of the church. He is blessed with his beautiful wife Rhonda and three daughters Natasha, Nichole and Natalie.

THIS BOOK IS DEDICATED TO...

all those emerging apostles and prophets
whom the Holy Spirit is using to bring
forth the glorious church

and to you,
The Reforming Generation!

IN THE MEMORY OF

Hesdey Alken

Amsterdam, The Netherlands
(1963-2000)

one of God's young lions

Governing Churches

"And I say also unto thee, That thou art Peter, and upon this rock I will build my church; and the gates of hell shall not prevail against it."

(Matthew 16:18)

CONTENTS

Apostles build, guide, govern, blast, establish, carry liberty, impart blessing, set, father, mature, set the pace, influence, train, send, launch, hear, say and do. We stand on the cutting edge of the restoration of the apostolic church.

With the restoration of apostolic ministry will come the rise of spiritual master builders and reformers who will rebuild the tabernacle of David and put in place a forgotten apostolic structural dimension.

The religious spirit will be one of the strongest opposing forces against the apostolic church in these last days.

Contents

cults, Greek mythology, idol worship and Judaism. Welcome to the apostolic church.

Chapter 8   107
Apostles, the Sent Ones

Apostolic anointings are pioneering, go first, vanguard anointings. Apostolic people are trail blazers in the realm of the spirit. They are the go first, cutting-edge gifts that many religious people are so uncomfortable with.

Chapter 9   115
Apostles & Territorial Opposition

Apostolic ministry is strategic, with purpose and design and will impact gateway cities with teams that have been prepared to meet the demonic representatives of territories.

Chapter 10   133
The Apostolic Company

Before we see the manifestation of the glorious church, we will have a structural change take place enabling us to reach our cities. That structural change will release apostolic companies.

Contents

Governing Churches

FOREWORD

Jonas Clark is an end-time apostolic reformer. This is evident in this book on the subject of apostolic ministry. We are presently seeing a restoration of the apostolic ministry to the worldwide church, and books like this will be necessary for leaders to embrace and walk in this anointing accurately. This is not just a theological exposition on the subject, but revelation from a leader that is implementing this strategy in the local church and expanding outward to touch the nations.

The current leadership of the church must embrace an apostolic, Antioch paradigm of building churches. This is the model that is emphasized in this book. Jonas Clark ministers this truth with conviction and boldness. There are no apologies in presenting truth. I love the conviction and boldness of the author in saying what needs to be said. There is no other way to attack the religious strongholds that have been built over generations by the enemy who hates and fears apostolic ministry.

Books like this need to be released in every region and territory. This will make preaching and teaching on the restoration of apostolic much easier. We will see the planting and building of Antioch churches in every region. The terminology used in this book will help leaders understand the concepts and truths that the Holy Spirit is releasing to the church. I would encourage leaders to preach these truths to their congregations and renew the minds of believers everywhere.

Ten years ago, there were very few books on this subject available. We are now seeing a release of books on the subject of apostolic ministry. This is the work of the Holy Spirit. I highly recommend Governing Churches and Antioch Apostles to the Body of Christ worldwide.

John Eckhardt,
September 2000

AUTHOR'S PREFACE

By picking up this book, you have demonstrated concrete evidence that the Spirit of God is drawing you this very moment into a great cause -- *the restoration of the apostolic church.*

When David ran to the battle line with a shout, his brothers challenged his motives for being there. Fear had crippled the army of God as they listened to the terrifying threats of the Philistine champion, Goliath. But David carried a different spirit. He looked around at the paralyzed men and boldly asked, "IS THERE NOT A CAUSE?" (1 Samuel 17:29). David was different than the other soldiers gathered on the battle field. The purpose of God filled him with boldness, zeal, passion and the desire to overcome.

Today there are thousands across the globe who feel like they just don't fit in. Some have been rejected and resisted for being too fervent, too bold, too zealous, too militant, too everything. Many are discontent, distressed, in debt and in search of identity and destiny (1 Samuel 22:1-2). Nevertheless there remains in them a cause, a mighty sword that can't be seen. They desire to let God's power be strong in them and see territories, cities and nations impacted by the power of

3

Governing Churches

God. "Who are they?" you ask. They are the coming apostolic reformers.

We certainly live in changing times and I am so excited about the future of the church. Right now the Spirit of God is pouring out a fresh understanding of the Word of God concerning the restoration of the apostolic church. The following pages will navigate through the white waters of religion and tradition as we discover the new apostolic reformation. You will also learn to recognize and relate to the apostolic ministry gifts as spiritual pioneers who are setting the stage for the manifestation of the glorious church.

It has been my prayer to capture and present to you in words...

the spirit of the apostle

and the coming glorious church.

Your partner,

Jonas Clark

PROPHETIC PRELUDE

Released at
The Global Cause Network of Churches
Inaugural Conference in Hallandale,
Florida

I heard the Lord say, "I am going to be releasing a new strategy into your hands. I'm causing My people to begin to walk with a new strategy and with a new insight even concerning ministry." The Lord said, "I'm going to re-educate you and re-teach you what it means to be a true minister of Christ, of what it means to be sent by Me."

The Lord says, "I'm going to change your motives, I'm going to change your focus, I'm going to change your orientation." The Lord said, "I'm thrusting you into something new. I'm releasing, even that apostolic anointing into the earth on those who are ready to receive it," says God. The Lord says, "As you're faithful and as you're committed to the cause that I'm releasing in the earth, regardless of what men think, I will bless you and I will use you to influence regions and nations and territories." And the Lord says, "This is a time of change in which My word is going out throughout all the earth, and many are saying, 'I will not change, I do not believe,' but those whose

5

hearts are open to that which I am releasing, I will give you the grace and I will give you the wisdom and I will give you the strategies whereby you will be able to break through and you will be able to see results that you have never seen before in your ministry," says God.

And the Lord says, "I will even put into your hands the destinies of entire nations and entire continents and entire cities and entire regions," says God. "I put the keys in your hand and whatever you bind on earth shall be bound in heaven and whatever you loose on earth shall be loosed in heaven, for behold I give you apostolic authority with that revelation," says God, "and I give you the keys which will unlock regions and territories," and the Lord said, "there shall come forth even a Macedonian call from the nations to say, 'Come over and help us.' They shall call for the teams who have linked themselves together in apostolic purpose and prophetic insight and anointing to be a blessing unto regions beyond," says God, "and even though men will not recognize you and even though some will not give you even the credit that is due," the Lord says, "I will even bless you and I will even reward you and I will even count you as one of My servants and one of My choice vessels in this hour." The Lord says, "To get ready for I am releasing new insight and new understandings and new revelations concerning My will and My purpose in the earth today."

And the Lord says, "I will begin to open up the scriptures in a new way and begin to cause you to see things that you have not seen before and even scriptures that you read before shall come alive and I shall give you new insight and I shall give you a depth of understanding and a depth of revelation that you have not known before. And I shall cause your hearts even to rejoice at the treasures that you shall find in My words," says God, "and you shall have a new joy and a new fervency. You shall preach with a new anointing and with a new zeal, you shall bring forth My truth into the earth," says God, "and I will cause a new excitement and a new joy to come alive in your hearts for I have given you My word in a new way and you shall preach it with a new depth, with a new understanding, with a new insight and you shall bring insight and revelation even to people in darkness," says God.

"You shall cause the eyes of the blind to be open and the ears of the deaf to be unstopped and they shall see My plan and My purpose and it shall come alive in the hearts of men and women throughout the globe," says God. "And I shall cause My light to come even as a sun that shines in the mid-day at its strength," says God, "I shall bring My light and My wisdom and My revelation to the four corners of the earth." And the Lord says, "I extend your line and I will extend your influence, and I extend your authority into places where you have never been before," says God, "and you shall go in but you shall not go in because of men. You shall go in because I will open the door for you and I will cause you to go in with authority and power and you shall go in and root up. Yes, you shall tear down, pull down, destroy, but you shall also build and plant," says God.

"You shall see My work flourish in places where there have been hindrances and blockages and obstructions," says God. "You shall be igniters of My glory and igniters of revival," says God. "I will give you a key and you shall ignite and you shall instigate My purposes and release My powers in different places," says God, for the Lord says, "This is a new day and a new season in the earth. So rise up and receive it, rise up and begin to go forth in it and as you do, you shall see success and breakthroughs in the places that I shall send you in the days to come," says the Spirit of the Living God.

Apostle John Eckhardt

CHAPTER 1
SOUNDS OF
THE APOSTOLIC
CHURCH

Apostles build, guide, govern, blast, establish, carry liberty, impart blessing, set, father, mature, set the pace, influence, train, send, launch, hear, say and do. We stand on the cutting edge of the restoration of the apostolic church.

We have been hearing from the prophets that the apostles are coming. I believe that the apostolic reforming spirit of God has already arrived. The word of God tells us of a restoration of all things before the return of the Lord. Many things are being restored in this hour and the restoration of the apostolic church is a major part of the fulfillment of that scripture. Scripture declares of Jesus, "Whom the heaven must receive until the times of restoration of all things, which God hath spoken by the mouth of all his holy prophets since the world began" (Acts 3:21 KJV).

Governing Churches

God is giving us little bits of prophetic insight into the restoration of the apostolic church. This book is but a meager glimpse into that truth. You might ask yourself these questions in regards to the restoration of all things and specifically the apostolic church:

> If there is a restoration of an apostolic church, then how can it be identified?
>
> What really is different about it?
>
> How would one clearly recognize it from others?

APOSTOLIC CHURCHES ARE VERY SENSITIVE TO THE SPIRITUAL CLIMATE AROUND THEM.

As we examine these questions, one of the most striking signs of apostolic churches is the spiritual climate of their meetings. When you walk in the door you can sense that something is different. The most amazing thing about this type of ministry is that...

Sounds Of The Apostolic Church

apostolic churches are very sensitive to the spiritual climate around them.

Because of the anointing upon them, they can aggressively contend with hard heavens and command spiritual change. Churches that carry an apostolic reforming spirit are churches that nurture and pastor people but do not neglect the spiritual climates of their territories. They know how to contend with the hard brazen heavens that hinder prayer, praise, liberty and the spiritual growth of the people. They know how to command spiritual gates to open that the King of Glory might come in.

Listen, and you will hear that even the music is different in their services. Why? Because apostolic music has more of a spiritual punch to it. It's the sound of authority. Their songs are not always nice mellow tunes, but are very commanding, decreeing, and proclaiming. They are songs that lift up and exalt Jesus while prophetically decreeing the will of the Lord.

What's going on?

Why are things so different?

Why so much change?

It's because we have entered apostolic times. Again, the word of God tells us about a time of great change that will take place before the coming of the Lord. We also know that times of restoration or change are always preceded by a reforming spirit as mentioned in Hebrews 9:10.

YOU CANNOT HAVE TIMES OF RESTORATION WITHOUT TIMES OF REFORMATION.

The word reformation is the Greek word *diorthosis* which means to straighten out thoroughly and to restore to its natural and normal condition. So we learn that...

you cannot have times of restoration without times of reformation.

The vehicle for this restoration of all things will be the reforming anointing of the apostolic church. So let's introduce a few of her characteristics.

REFORMATION CHURCHES

Reforming churches are governing churches. By that I mean that they are very confrontational in the realm of the spirit. They have a high level of spiritual boldness. They confront and tear down religious idolatry, religious form and vain religious traditions. They give identity to those who were not received because of what they carry spiritually. They are highly committed and dedicated to advancing the cause of Jesus. They don't ignore, but rather attack the giants in the land. The giants of ...

religion

divination

racism

witchcraft

anti-christ

Jezebel

Reforming churches build their ministries on Spirit life rather than social religious programs. They are the working churches with a pursuing spirit, often known to be bold but who carry and impart spiritual strength (Ezekiel 1:24,43:2). Apostolic churches have fervent, even militant sounding prayer lives because they believe that fervent prayer makes much of God's power available (James 5:16).

Reforming churches carry spiritual authority and are not afraid to use it. They have a vision for reaching all nations for Christ. They minister with fresh prophetic insight. They are order and divine flow people who can command dormant gifts to stir and come alive! They know the word of God *and* the ways of God. Reforming churches...

build
guide
govern
blast
establish
carry liberty
impart blessing
set
father
mature
set the pace
influence
train
send
launch
hear

say
do

We stand on the cutting edge of the restoration of the apostolic reforming *(diorthosis)* church.

ROAR OUT OF ZION

Let me also repeat a prophetic decree that the Spirit of God gave me in regards to a prelude to the greatest awaking the church as ever seen -- *the roar of Zion.*

> "The restored apostolic church will usher in the last great revival. This great revival will be carried on the wings of the roar of Zion. This great roar of Zion is the forerunning to the most prominent outpouring of the Holy Spirit since the book of Acts. It will be the bench mark to the greatest awakening toward God and will eclipse anything that we have ever seen in church history."

Some would ask, "What is this roar of Zion that will usher in the last great revival?" The roar of Zion is that great collective voice of unity in prayer, praise, purpose, and faith that collectively is like the sound of many waters. It is the working together of all five ministry anointings (Ephesians 4:11). Scripture declares, "The Lord also shall roar out of Zion, and utter his voice from Jerusalem; and the heavens and the earth shall shake: but the Lord will be the hope of his people, and the strength of the children of Israel" (Joel 3:16). Get ready for a mighty roar of the Spirit.

APOSTOLIC CHURCHES HAVE FERVENT, EVEN MILITANT SOUNDING PRAYER LIVES BECAUSE THEY BELIEVE THAT FERVENT PRAYER MAKES MUCH OF GOD'S POWER AVAILABLE.

This roar of Zion will be carried on the back of the restored apostolic church. We are beginning to see, hear and experience little outbreaks of this roar of Zion heard in the sound of prayer throughout the nations. One of the greatest indications of the restoration of the apostolic reforming church is the sound of prayer and praise when you enter their presence.

SOUND OF
APOSTOLIC PRAYER

This sound of apostolic prayer is distinct. You can tell that there is something different about an apostolic reforming church when you hear the sound of prayer in their midst. What is it? They have lifted up their voice - not only in an increasing level of noise, but also in the fervor of apostolic and spiritual authority. *Strong prayer and praise is an indication of the presence of apostolic strength and authority.*

What you are hearing is strength in prayer and fervency in praise. This spiritual climate results in a spiritual liberty that the Spirit of God loves to flow in. There is also a militant aggression that is high level in effectiveness. The word declares that the effectual fervent prayer of a righteous man avails much (James 5:16). How much more so for a fervent church, the forerunners and carriers of revival? The word says that God will present to himself a glorious church (Ephesians 5:27). But...

can there be a glorious church without prayer?

17

Can there be a glorious church without strength, praise, and liberty?

PRAYER, PRAISE AND LIBERTY

The foundational element missing in the church today that will be heard by this great roar of Zion is the spirit of prayer, praise, and liberty. This will be the main thrust of the reforming apostolic restoration that will finally free God's people and release them into ministry. Prayer is the prominent thing that Jesus said would identify his house; "My house shall be called the house of prayer" (Matthew 21:13).

The great revivalist Charles Finney speaking about prayer said, "The Spirit in the hearts of saints is preeminently a spirit of prayer, and of course to restrain prayer always quenches the Spirit."

Thousands of people pray everyday, yet the spirit of prayer is the one thing that is missing. Why is it missing? Because one must hunger and thirst after it. Strong apostolic prayer won't come to you; one must go after it. "Then shall ye call upon me, and ye shall go and pray unto me, and I will hearken unto you. {13} And ye shall seek me, and find *me,* when ye shall search for me with all your heart" (Jeremiah 29:12-13 KJV).

Spiritual liberty must be fought for with diligent fervor (Galations 5:1). It is the spirit of prayer that will usher in the new reforming songs that have been prophesied. These songs...

have a different sound

are filled with Spirit life

carry His presence

prepare the way for greater spiritual capacity

It is another realm beloved (John 14:2), and from these new songs will come a high level of apostolic strength into the people. The result will be the roar of Zion coming out of the church that will sweep the earth with God's glory. This roar of Zion will lift up the Name of Jesus as the Most High. This spirit of prayer and praise will...

equip, release and manifest the sons of God.

Are you ready to discover the new apostolic anointing?

Governing Churches

In the following pages we will see the critical importance of the local church in the restoration process as a place that soon will be transformed into the gathering place of the sent ones. Let's take a look at the church Jesus is building.

Sounds Of The Apostolic Church

SUMMARY: SOUNDS OF THE APOSTOLIC CHURCH

☐ Apostolic churches are very sensitive to the spiritual climate around them.

☐ The word reformation is the Greek word *diorthosis* which means to straighten out thoroughly and to restore to its natural and normal condition.

☐ You cannot have times of restoration without times of reformation.

☐ The vehicle for this restoration of all things will be the reforming anointing of the apostolic church.

☐ Apostolic churches attack the giants in the land of religion, divination, racism, witchcraft, anti-christ, and Jezebel.

☐ Apostolic churches have fervent, even militant sounding prayer lives because they believe that fervent prayer makes much of God's power available (James 5:16).

Governing Churches

☐ Strong prayer and praise is an indication of the presence of apostolic strength and apostolic authority.

☐ Prayer is the prominent thing that Jesus said would identify his house; "My house shall be called the house of prayer" (Matthew 21:13).

CHAPTER 2
THE CHURCH JESUS IS BUILDING

With the restoration of apostolic ministry will come the rise of spiritual master builders and reformers who will rebuild the tabernacle of David and put in place a forgotten apostolic structural dimension.

SEAT OF AUTHORITY

If I was to ask what is the most powerful seat of authority on the earth today, some would say that it is the United States Federal Government, the Supreme Court, or perhaps even a United Europe. Some would say that this seat of authority would be found in education, banking, Wall Street, or perhaps within the ranks of the media. However...

the most powerful seat of authority on the earth today is Jesus' church.

Even with this solid conclusion it is interesting to note that the church of Jesus Christ is often the most overlooked, persecuted, harassed, mocked, and ignored institution; yet, it remains the only seat of authority divinely authorized to carry a governmental, God-ordained anointing (Isaiah 9:6-7).

Throughout history kingdoms have risen to great levels of influence through natural government only to find themselves crashing to the ground in utter rubble and decay. However, the church of Jesus Christ presses on having survived throughout history and has, in fact, increased from generation to generation. Jesus prophesied, "I will build my church and the gates of hell shall not prevail." The Bible teaches us that Jesus will return and when he does it will be for a church without spot or wrinkle, a glorious church.

> "That he might present it to himself a glorious church, not having spot, or wrinkle, or any such thing; but that it should be holy and without blemish." (Ephesians 5:27 KJV)

THE GLORIOUS CHURCH

Sadly, we see little evidence today of this glorious victorious church that Jesus prophesied about. What we see mostly is a religious church, full of dead religious programs and the traditions of men. Though we may not see this glorious church in her fullness, there does remain

The Church Jesus Is Building

a fully dedicated remnant that is standing ready for the Master's use.

So where is this glorious church? To find her we must take a journey together and look for a church within a church.

Let's take a deeper look at the restoration of the apostolic church which God is using to make a way for the structure and the appearing of this glorious church. The restoration of apostolic ministry heralds the rise of spiritual master builders and reformers who will rebuild the tabernacle of David and put in place the forgotten apostolic structural dimension necessary to impact the world for Jesus Christ. Scripture declares, "After this I will return, and will build again the tabernacle of David, which is fallen down; and I will build again the ruins thereof, and I will set it up" (Acts 15:16 KJV).

Presently a paradigm shift is moving us away from the traditional understanding of the function and structure of the church, a "pastoral, teacher only" model of ministry into an "apostolic, gathering-to-send," structure of ministry. *The success of apostolic ministry will not be determined by how many people fill seats in an auditorium but rather how many are being sent.*

MASTER BUILDERS

The word says that the church is, "built upon the foundation of the apostles and prophets, Jesus Christ himself being the chief corner stone" (Ephesians 2:20 KJV).

It's very important to understand that when a building is built, the foundation that the structure rests upon must be solid and able to withstand the weight of the building. In other words the foundation that supports the building must be put solidly in place before the building goes up. If not, the weight of the building will crush the foundation and the building will collapse.

The ministry gifts of apostles and prophets are divinely set by Jesus as governmental in calling and spiritual capacity and are the very gifts which the Holy Spirit will use to lay the foundation for the building of the glorious church in these last days. We refer to those whom God uses to lay a spiritual foundation as the restored apostolic master builders. These master builders will ...

> be filled with the revelation of divine strategies to fulfill the Great Commission of reaching the world with the gospel of Jesus Christ.

The Church Jesus Is Building

be generals and commanders of an army of believers who have matured from childhood to sons, who are made ready to be sent into the harvest fields of this world.

teach the church the value of being interrelated, networkers, who make a way for apostolic direction, empowerment and sending.

possess a willingness to entertain new possibilities, and a readiness to explore unfamiliar practices.

be the apostolic fathers to a fatherless generation.

lead the church as front-line, cutting-edge, battlefield soldiers and pioneers for Christ preparing the church for a glorious future.

be the coming reformers who will oppose false doctrines, false religious structures, apathy, lukewarmness, demonic spiritual governments and false religious voices with a passionate spirit not seen since the days of The Great Reformation.

Get ready for the rise of the apostolic glorious church -- the governing church.

A NEW
MODEL OF MINISTRY

The current structure or model of church operations is centered around a pastoral paradigm. A paradigm is an example of ministry that serves as a model or pattern. It's astonishing, but the word pastor, (Greek, *poimen*) is only mentioned once in the entire New Testament. "And he gave some, apostles; and some, prophets; and some, evangelists; and some, pastors and teachers" (Ephesians 4:11 KJV).

Though we only see the word pastor, *poimen,* once in scripture, we have used it to create a model of how ministry is supposed to function and have made it our current pattern, understanding or paradigm. In reality we have created a structure of church services that is designed to gather, entertain, and baby-sit immature believers. Moreover, we actually call it pastoral, loving, and caring!

Some churches have hirelings as caretakers that God never called nor sent. These hirelings have been selected by some pulpit committee chaired by business men who were pre-qualified according to their financial status. The

28

hirelings then become the paid overseers of religious day care centers.

It is important for me to say that I am certainly not anti-church nor anti-pastor. I am strongly supportive of the local church with a set leader who is God-called provided the pattern of ministry is understood biblically. "Let the LORD, the God of the spirits of all flesh, set a man over the congregation" (Numbers 27:16 KJV). I'm a pastor myself, and I have not missed a church service in over sixteen years. Local meetings are very important for believers -- Jesus himself supported them. "And he came to Nazareth, where he had been brought up: and, as his custom was, he went into the synagogue on the Sabbath day, and stood up for to read" (Luke 4:16 KJV).

RELIGIOUS SYSTEMS

We've had two thousand years to reach this world for Jesus. Even in the time of profound technological advancements in communication, we still have not reached the world with the gospel. We know that this gospel of the kingdom must be preached in all the world as a witness before our Lord returns (Matthew 24:14).

So what's the problem? Could it be that we have created a religious system that in effect has caused us to be ineffective?

Governing Churches

Have we become so program oriented that we have bound ourselves in a powerless religious system? Have we so structured our ministries that we have created a religious form? Have we locked the Holy Spirit out of the church?

Without Holy Spirit-led meetings, it's easy to pattern our ministries into a religious form. We simply look at the current fad and copy it thereby allowing it to form some sort of structure or pattern. I don't want to sound anti-orderly, but many times we are so structured that we miss the point and purpose of our gathering ourselves together.

BLESS ME ONLY

In a religious context, church can become geared around a Sunday morning collection of people for an "hour of power." This is where you come in to church...

sing a few songs

hear a song special

listen to announcements

pay one's tithes

The Church Jesus Is Building

listen to a simple, non-compelling sermon or motivational message

receive your blessing

have a closing prayer

go home and wait for the next week of the same old same old.

In this setting everything is focused to climax in this one hour period. So inadvertently we create a system of "consumer only Christians" whose only purpose in coming to church is to receive. To receive the best in music and teaching with the finale of being prayed for to receive one's breakthrough. Please understand me. I am not at all against music, preaching, prayer, or breakthrough, but let's go a little further.

A religious structure of church services can create a "bless me only," event-oriented, entertainment model of services. Church then becomes a place where people become spectators only and are never released to do anything.

In order to gather numbers and fill chairs many churches have moved into...

entertainment

program services

Governing Churches

comedy

ritual

seeker-friendliness

consumer Christianity

franchised ministry

A franchise ministry is simply a cookie cutter of another ministry that has no Spirit life design. Because of this, we inadvertently have created a non-challenging, humanistic, consumer minded, religious system that is being promulgated each week throughout the world.

Today hundreds of churches are closing because they are refusing to let go of this old model of bless me only Christianity. I submit to you, that the Holy Spirit is challenging this concept of ministry and is now releasing a reforming voice into the earth to address this issue.

Our answer to effective ministry will not be found in church growth seminars based on a humanistic effort to get people to pencil Christ into their busy weekly schedules. Effective ministry will come by the guidance of the Holy Spirit, revelation from the Word of God and hard work.

The Church Jesus Is Building

The church was never intended to be built around a bless me only model of Christianity. It was designed to be built upon the foundational leadership of apostles and prophets with Jesus Christ himself as the chief corner stone.

A. W. Tozer declared, "How tragic that we in this dark day have had our seeking done for us by our teachers. Everything is made to center upon the initial act of 'accepting' Christ (a term, incidentally, which is not found in the Bible) and we are not expected thereafter to crave any further revelation of God to our souls."

Apostolic ministry gifts are spiritual master builders. As Paul says, "According to the grace of God which is given unto me, as a wise master builder, I have laid the foundation, and another buildeth thereon. But let every man take heed how he buildeth thereupon" (1 Corinthians 3:10 KJV).

My prayer is for the manifestation of this grace once again to rest on the church. The following chapters will be challenging to some but will unfold an apostolic structure where every believer moves past a bless me only, consumer mind-set of Christianity and ministry, into a build me, mature me, prepare me and send me concept of ministry.

The pattern of an apostolic structure can be found in the book of Acts. As we continue on our journey to discover the new apostolic reformation we will begin to unfold the pattern of a truly apostolic church.

The Church Jesus Is Building

SUMMARY: THE CHURCH JESUS IS BUILDING

☐ The church is the most powerful seat of authority in the earth (Isaiah 9:6-7).

☐ Jesus is going to return for a glorious church. (Ephesians 5:27)

☐ The church is built upon the foundation of the apostles and prophets with Jesus himself as chief corner stone. (Ephesians 2:20)

☐ The word pastor, (Greek *poimen*) is only mentioned once in the New Testament in Ephesians 4:11.

☐ It was the custom of Jesus to go to the synagogue on the Sabbath day. (Luke 4:16)

Governing Churches

CHAPTER 3
APOSTLES & RELIGIOUS PERSECUTION

The religious spirit will be one of the strongest opposing forces against the apostolic church in these last days.

Our travel into discovering the new apostolic reformation begins with the believers who were scattered everywhere because of the religious persecution that arose against the church in Jerusalem.

"Now they which were scattered abroad upon the persecution that arose about Stephen traveled as far as Phenice, and Cyprus, and Antioch, preaching the word to none but unto the Jews only" (Acts 11:19 KJV).

Stephen, a man full of faith and power, did great wonders and miracles among the people and found himself being challenged by the leaders of a religious stronghold. The spirit of religion is always frightened by those who are anointed by the Holy Spirit because...

37

religious spirits sit in seats of authority that do not belong to them.

To hold on to their man-centered positions of authority they will mount up an offensive attack on those who carry God's governing anointing. "And Stephen, full of faith and power, did great wonders and miracles among the people. {9} Then there arose certain of the synagogue, which is called the synagogue of the Libertines, and Cyrenians, and Alexandrians, and of them of Cilicia and of Asia, disputing with Stephen. {10} And they were not able to resist the wisdom and the spirit by which he spake" (Acts 6:8-10 KJV).

RELIGIOUS SPIRITS HAVE A DARK ABILITY TO PROVOKE TO ANGER AND STIR UP OTHERS AGAINST THE THINGS OF GOD.

These men were unable to resist the wisdom and the spirit by which Stephen spoke, so they stirred up the people, elders, and scribes of this self-appointed religious bunch against Stephen. Religious spirits have a dark ability to provoke to anger and stir up others against the things of God.

RELIGIOUS OPPOSITION AND PERSECUTION IS EVIDENCE OF ENTERING INTO AN APOSTOLIC DIMENSION OF MINISTRY.

"Then they suborned (furnished) men, which said, We have heard him speak blasphemous words against Moses, and against God. {12} And they stirred up the people, and the elders, and the scribes, and came upon him, and caught him, and brought him to the council" (Acts 6:11-12 KJV).

Believers in the word of God regularly meet either religious persecution or occult opposition as soon as they begin to obey the Holy Spirit. Here, in typical fashion, the religious spirits set up false witnesses to build their case against Stephen, a devout man who loved God.

It is important to remember that Stephen stirred up trouble while ministering on the streets, not in the church services. Religious opposition and persecution is evidence of entering into an apostolic dimension of ministry.

The apostolic mantel of authority will expose a religious spirit every time. "And set up false witnesses, which said, This man ceaseth not to speak blasphemous words against this holy place, and the law: {14} For we have heard him say, that this Jesus of Nazareth shall destroy this place, and shall change the customs which Moses delivered to us. {15} And all that sat in the council, looking stedfastly on him, saw his face as it had been the face of an angel" (Acts 6:13-15 KJV).

RELIGIOUS ANGER

As Stephen preached a powerful anointed message to those assembled at this religious council they were cut to the heart, so much so, that they gnashed their teeth in furious anger. Imagine, these grown men, elders of Jerusalem, who were unable to control their murderous emotions. Why? "When they heard these things, they were cut to the heart, and they gnashed on him with their teeth" (Acts 7:54 KJV).

Stephen being full of the Holy Ghost had an open vision as he saw the glory of God and Jesus standing at God's right hand. The Holy Spirit never abandons those who stand fast against ungodly religious opposition. "But he, being full of the Holy Ghost, looked up stedfastly into heaven, and saw the glory of God, and Jesus standing on the right hand of God, {56} And said, Behold, I see the heavens opened, and the Son of man standing on the right hand of God" (Acts 7:55-56 KJV).

RELIGIOUS PERSECUTION ALWAYS RESULTS IN THE ADVANCEMENT OF MINISTRY.

Stephen, with his last breath and a loud voice, asked the Lord not to lay this sin to their charge. Then he stepped victoriously from this world into glory.

The religious spirit that Stephen faced was a murdering spirit. "And they stoned Stephen, calling upon God, and saying, Lord Jesus, receive my spirit. {60} And he kneeled down, and cried with a loud voice, Lord, lay not this sin to their charge. And when he had said this, he fell asleep" (Acts 7:59-60 KJV). The religious spirit will be one of the strongest opposing forces against the apostolic church in these last days (Matt 23:31). The religious church is a man-motivated, dead, works-oriented, soulish, carnal church with only a form of godliness; but without Holy Ghost leadership, revelation, inspiration and power.

Little did Stephen know that God was causing all things to work together for good. Every time the church is persecuted it grows, multiplies, and is strengthened.

After the vicious murder of Stephen in the name of Jehovah, the believers were "scattered abroad and went every where preaching the word" (Acts 8:4 KJV). Religious persecution always results in the advancement of ministry.

In the next chapter we will look at what happened after these believers were driven out of their comfortable church in Jerusalem and forced to hit the streets with gospel power.

Apostles & Religious Persecution

SUMMARY: APOSTLES & RELIGIOUS PERSECUTION

☐ Stephen ministered to people on the streets outside the church.

☐ Religious persecution is evidence of entering an apostolic dimension.

☐ The spirit of religion is always frightened by those who are anointed by the Holy Spirit.

☐ The religious spirit will be one of the strongest opposing forces against the apostolic church in these last days.

☐ Religious spirits have an ability to provoke to anger and stir up others.

☐ Stephen was murdered by a religious spirit.

☐ The religious church is a man-motivated, dead works-oriented, soulish, carnal church with a form of godliness, but without Holy Ghost inspiration and power (2 Timothy 3:5).

43

Governing Churches

☐ Religious persecution always results in an advancement in ministry.

CHAPTER 4
THE ANTIOCH APOSTLES

The apostolic model of churches will be full of believers that conquer their own prejudices. Prejudice is a preconceived and usually unfavorable idea or opinion of others. It leads to a hatred or intolerance of other races or cultures.

L ittle is said in the word of God about what happened in the local meetings of the church, but there is a lot said about what happened after the meetings were over. Let's find out why.

Now some of those believers who were scattered from Jerusalem by the murdering religious spirits came to the city of Antioch.

"Now they which were scattered abroad upon the persecution that arose about Stephen traveled as far as Phenice, and Cyprus, and Antioch, preaching the word to none but unto the Jews only" (Acts 11:19 KJV).

ANTIOCH

Antioch was about three hundred miles north of Jerusalem. At its height it probably had a population of a half million people. It was the third largest city in the Roman Empire. The two only other cities that were larger were Rome and Alexandria in Egypt. Antioch was a cosmopolitan city, rich with splendors from around the world and full of many cultures. Antioch can be likened to a spiritual gateway city of utmost importance. It was also a city with a large Jewish population and was divided by walls into four quadrants, Greek, Syrian, African, and Jewish. It is known today as Antakiya in Turkey, a town of thirty-five thousand.

CULTURALLY BOUND

In the beginning the fugitive and emigrant believers from Jerusalem preached Jesus unto the Jews only. But one day something historic happened, some men of Cyprus and Cyrene began to preach the gospel to the Gentiles. This was unheard of indeed! Gentiles were unclean and certainly considered outside the covenant blessings of Abraham.

The Antioch Apostles

"And some of them were men of Cyprus and Cyrene, which, when they were come to Antioch, spake unto the Grecians, preaching the Lord Jesus" (Acts 11:20 KJV).

THE APOSTOLIC MODEL OF GOVERNING CHURCHES WILL BE FULL OF BELIEVERS THAT CONQUER THEIR OWN PREJUDICES.

About this same time, the Apostle Peter was sent by the angel of the Lord to the house of Cornelius, a Roman centurion of the Italian band and a Gentile. Peter's message was filled with breakthrough revelation to Cornelius' household, "of a truth I perceive that God is no respecter of persons, but in every nation he that feareth him and worketh righteousness is accepted with him" (Acts 10:34-35). With Peter's visit, Cornelius' house was to be the first Gentile gathering of believers.

"While Peter yet spake these words, the Holy Ghost fell on all them which heard the word. {45} And

47

they of the circumcision which believed were astonished, as many as came with Peter, because that on the Gentiles also was poured out the gift of the Holy Ghost. {46} For they heard them speak with tongues, and magnify God. Then answered Peter, {47} Can any man forbid water, that these should not be baptized, which have received the Holy Ghost as well as we? {48} And he commanded them to be baptized in the name of the Lord. Then prayed they him to tarry certain days" (Acts 10:44-48 KJV).

Here we see the carrying out of the scriptures, "Behold my servant, whom I uphold; mine elect, in whom my soul delighteth; I have put my spirit upon him: he shall bring forth judgment to the Gentiles" (Isaiah 42:1 KJV) and "For from the rising of the sun even unto the going down of the same my name shall be great among the Gentiles; and in every place incense shall be offered unto my name, and a pure offering: for my name shall be great among the heathen, saith the LORD of hosts" (Malachi 1:11 KJV).

These scriptures should be good news and encouragement for those of you who have a heart for the hard spiritual hearts of Italy. God sent his apostle, Peter, to a

Gentile Italian and poured out his Holy Ghost power. He will do it again.

BIRTH OF A NEW TESTAMENT APOSTOLIC CHURCH

The city of Antioch was also experiencing something powerful; God was birthing a New Testament apostolic church. As the believers preached to the Gentiles in the city, faith began to rise in these pagans, giving way to conviction of sin, repentance and salvation in the Lord Jesus Christ, "for the hand of the Lord was upon them and a great number believed, and turned unto the Lord" (Acts 11:21 KJV).

It is awesome to see what faithful believers can do when they obey the Great Commission. "And he said unto them, Go ye into all the world, and preach the gospel to every creature" (Mark 16:15 KJV).

ETHNIC DIVISION AND PREJUDICE

The Antioch believers saw the ethnic division in their town as a barrier that had to be overcome. Antioch's town was made up of Greeks, Syrians, Africans, and Jews. The preaching of the gospel broke down these powerful walls of separation. The apostolic model of governing churches will be full of believers that conquer their own prejudices. Prejudice is a preconceived and usually unfavorable idea or opinion of others. It leads to a hatred or intolerance of other races or cultures.

Jesus told his disciples that they would have to witness to Samaria before going to the uttermost. The Jews and the Samaritans were at odds with each other. The Samaritans' heresy was to claim Mount Gerizim as the true place of worship while the Jews chose Mount Zion in Jerusalem. This caused a great division and an extreme prejudice among them. *We cannot reach our goal of preaching the gospel of Jesus Christ throughout the nations of the world until we conquer our own prejudice.*

There can be no room in our hearts for this type of division.

> "For he is our peace, who hath made both one, and hath broken down the middle wall of partition between us; {15} Having abolished in his flesh the enmity, even the law of commandments contained in ordinances; for to make in himself of twain one new man, so making

peace; {16} And that he might reconcile both unto God in one body by the cross, having slain the enmity thereby: {17} And came and preached peace to you which were afar off, and to them that were nigh. {18} For through him we both have access by one Spirit unto the Father. {19} Now therefore ye are no more strangers and foreigners, but fellowcitizens with the saints, and of the household of God; {20} And are built upon the foundation of the apostles and prophets, Jesus Christ himself being the chief corner stone; {21} In whom all the building fitly framed together groweth unto an holy temple in the Lord: {22} In whom ye also are builded together for an habitation of God through the Spirit" (Ephesians 2:14-22 KJV).

MULTIPLICITY OF CULTURAL LEADERSHIP

The leadership at Antioch was multi-cultural in structure and is a pattern for apostolic churches to follow today. In order to reach every culture in our cities we have to do something different...

we must be staffed with a multiplicity of cultural leaders.

I met a professional once who had on her office walls many newspaper articles about her efforts to reconcile the races. She also had received many awards and had been invited to many events to speak about her thoughts on uniting different cultures. I remember sitting in her office as she told me of all the city officials who wanted to talk with her. She really wanted me to comment on her efforts. I looked around and saw all the awards hanging on the walls for all her patrons to see. But one thing really stood out to me as I took a close look at her employees. After a while I told her that I thought what she wanted to do was great, but one thing really puzzled me. "What?" she asked. "All your staff is from one tribe -- white," I replied. It is not enough to talk about uniting cultures. There must be a visible change. Adding staff from various cultures helps accomplish this task.

We must put action with our words.

Often times in Europe, churches of one culture will not worship with those of another culture. I have seen African churches separated, not because of color, but because of tribal differences. Nigerians seldom worship with those from Ghana. The French speaking people of Belgium seldom worship with the Flemish speaking people in the same country. In South Florida the Spanish speaking Cubans seldom worship with the Spanish speaking people from Nicaragua. The list of comparisons could continue on and on. But just as it did in Antioch, all of this is about to change with the restoration of the apostolic church. The walls that separate us are about to tumble down.

GOOD NEWS TRAVELS

Even with such a great accomplishment as this in Antioch, the Holy Spirit had much more in His plan. He wanted to take the Antioch Christians from a believers only anointing to the empowerment of a sending, apostolic governing church.

It wasn't long before the good news in Antioch found its way to the apostles and the church in Jerusalem. Up until this time there was only one New Testament church and it was in the city of Jerusalem. After hearing about the mighty breakthrough of believers in Antioch they sent Barnabas to them for further investigation.

"Then tidings of these things came unto the ears of the church which was in Jerusalem: and they sent forth Barnabas, that he should go as far as Antioch" (Acts 11:22 KJV).

BARNABAS ARRIVES IN ANTIOCH

When Barnabas arrived in Antioch he saw God moving mightily upon the believers' lives. The word says that, "Who, when he came, and had seen the grace of God, was glad, and exhorted them all, that with purpose of heart they would cleave unto the Lord. {24} For he was a good man, and full of the Holy Ghost and of faith: and much people was added unto the Lord" (Acts 11:23-24 KJV).

THE HUNGER OF BELIEVERS IS A VERY IMPORTANT DYNAMIC IN THE FLOW OF REVELATION THAT COMES FROM GOD'S MINISTERS.

What did Barnabas see? He saw joy, fervency, spiritual hunger, a church that was behind in no spiritual gift (1 Corinthians 12), and a people willing to share their faith with others outside of a religious setting. Apostolic grace is visible.

BARNABAS' SPIRITUAL CAPACITY

Barnabas, after arriving in Antioch began to exhort the believers. The word exhort means to...

comfort

console

encourage

build up

and to teach.

It indicates strength and tenderness.

The Greek word exhorted (*parakaleo*) gives us an indication of the spiritual capacity in which Barnabas operated at the time. In the light of this scripture and the reputation of Barnabas as being the son of encouragement, his dominate anointing after being sent forth from Jerusalem was that of a teacher. However, it is possible that Barnabas was also very prophetic.

Barnabas' real name was Joses. He was surnamed Barnabas by the apostles which means the son of consolation (Acts 4:36). The Greek word consolation is *paraklesis* and it is the same word used to describe a prophetic utterance. "But he that prophesieth speaketh unto men to edification, and exhortation, and comfort" (1 Corinthians 14:3 KJV).

The Antioch church was about to take another step in the unfolding times of reformation. They were paving the way for an apostolic church.

BELIEVERS RESPOND TO BARNABAS

Barnabas was surely a tenderhearted and kind man. Those who were assembled together in Antioch received him with great joy. How we respond to apostolic leadership is very important to our spiritual advancement. They recognized Barnabas as a sent one, honored him as a man of God with governmental capacity as a teacher, and valued his encouraging leadership. Apostolic churches recognize the anointing and calling of others.

These Antioch believers received Barnabas into their midst as a sent one.

The Antioch Apostles

They honored him, put a demand on his anointing, and allowed him to encourage and teach them.

In many churches today there are those that don't recognize that which is being carried spiritually and imparted by the man of God. The hunger of believers is a very important dynamic in the flow of revelation that comes from God's ministers. Where there is no hunger, there is little to no revelation. But wherever you find hungry people you will find much spiritual insight and revelation flowing.

As we continue we are going to look at what happens when apostolic leadership is received by hungry people.

Governing Churches

☐ The Antioch believers saw the ethnic division in their town as a barrier that had to be overcome. Preaching of the gospel broke down these powerful walls of separation.

☐Prejudice is a preconceived and usually unfavorable idea or opinion of others. It leads to a hatred or intolerance of other races or cultures.

☐Apostolic churches will be full of believers that conquer their own prejudices.

☐ The leadership at Antioch was multi-cultural in structure. Apostolic churches are staffed with a multiplicity of cultural leaders.

CHAPTER 5
SEARCHING
FOR APOSTOLIC
INCREASE

Apostolic gifts recognize and pull on the spiritual gifts of others that might add to the churches' effectiveness.

The anointing on Barnabas to encourage and teach caused the Antioch church to increase in size and spirituality. He may have been content with this increase, but the Spirit of God was not going to build a pastoral only, exhorting only, encouraging only, bless me only, maintenance only church, but an apostolic governing and sending forth church.

Barnabas himself was an apostolic gift who was seeking after an apostolic increase. Barnabas, an incredible man, recognized the need for help. He was the first man of influence to open his heart to Saul of Tarsus when all of Jerusalem wanted to kill him (Acts 9:20-31). He remembered Saul's great encounter with the Lord on the road to Damascus and went to Tarsus to seek him out. Apostolic leadership is always looking for willing hearts whom they can recruit and equip for service.

PRESSING INTO APOSTOLIC INCREASE

I really admire Barnabas for this action. He was a man who knew his own limitations and pressed into God for increase. He recognized that the church at Antioch was not his, but belonged to Jesus Christ, the head. He was willing to allow the Holy Spirit to take this church to a level of effectiveness where no one had been before. Barnabas, like all apostles, was indeed a spiritual pioneer. Apostolic gifts are spiritual pioneers who, through faith, are willing to press into the unknown and the unfamiliar.

APOSTOLIC MINISTRY GIFTS ARE CHAMPIONS OF COOPERATION AND NOT COMPETITION.

Barnabas was truly a great man and effective leader. His heart to seek out Saul speaks of a high level of spiritual maturity, identity, and security in his life. Apostolic ministry gifts are champions of cooperation and not competition.

As we will learn later, apostolic ministry gifts are truly masters of teamwork. Wisdom knows that we need each other and apostolic leaders understand the importance of one another.

HAVING A BURDEN FOR THE ADVANCEMENT AND SPIRITUAL GROWTH OF THE LOCAL CHURCH IS A SIGN OF APOSTOLIC CALLING.

LAYING HOLD OF A MANTEL

"Then departed Barnabas to Tarsus, for to seek Saul" (Acts 11:25 KJV). Barnabas left Antioch on his quest to Tarsus to seek out Saul. This Greek word seek (*anazeteo*) indicates that it was not easy for Barnabas to find Saul. Being obedient to follow the leading of the Holy Spirit requires the use of much diligence *(anazeteo)* in the pursuit of a spiritual mantel. Apostolic gifts know how to press through obstacles and never give up.

The context of this verse is telling us that Barnabas, through diligent pursuit, laid hold on Saul's spiritual mantel. It was a hunger for what Paul carried in the Spirit that Barnabas sought. Apostolic leaders recognize the anointing on others, seek additional spiritual gifts, and lay hold on spiritual mantels that might add effectiveness and spiritual strength to the local church.

Having a burden for the advancement and spiritual growth of the local church is a sign of apostolic calling. Apostolic gifts are not afraid to pursue and go after that which the church needs to mature. Barnabas didn't look to the church in Jerusalem for help with the Gentile church. He perceived that what Saul carried in the Spirit was needed at Antioch and he went after it.

GOSPEL TO THE UNCIRCUMCISED

The Apostle Paul gives us some insight into his calling toward the Gentiles that perhaps Barnabas had seen.

"But contrariwise, when they saw that the gospel of the

uncircumcision was committed unto me, as the gospel of the circumcision was unto Peter; {8} (For he that wrought effectually in Peter to the apostleship of the circumcision, the same was mighty in me toward the Gentiles:) {9} And when James, Cephas, and John, who seemed to be pillars, perceived the grace that was given unto me, they gave to me and Barnabas the right hands of fellowship; that we should go unto the heathen, and they unto the circumcision. {10} Only they would that we should remember the poor; the same which I also was forward to do" (Galations 2:7-10 KJV).

Barnabas, upon finding Saul, surely filled him in on all the fabulous and exciting things that the Spirit of God was doing in Antioch among the Gentile believers. I can just picture them both filled with prayer, wonderment and expectation as they traveled that dusty Roman road on their way to Antioch.

SAUL IN ANTIOCH

Saul was born in Tarsus but later brought up in Jerusalem. He was a Jew who was also born a Roman citizen, which means that his father, who was a Pharisee, must have been a Roman citizen. Paul was a tentmaker by trade and was trained under the prominent Rabbi Gamaliel (Acts 22:3).

THE MOST PROMINENT GIFTS IN THE NEW TESTAMENT CHURCH WERE APOSTLES AND IN THE LAST DAYS IT WILL BE THE SAME.

Before Saul's conversion, he had a zealous religious spirit. He witnessed Stephen's brutal murder and was passionately opposed to Christianity in the name of Jehovah. However, Saul had a dramatic encounter with the Lord on the road to Damascus that changed his life forever (Acts 9:1-30). Whenever one has a supernatural encounter with the presence of God and His anointing he is changed into another man (1 Samuel 10:6).

SET IN THE CHURCH

"And when he had found him, he brought him unto Antioch. And it came to pass, that a whole year they assembled themselves with the church, and taught much people. And the disciples were called Christians first in Antioch" (Acts 11:26 KJV).

Something mighty was about to take place in Antioch. Barnabas brought Saul back with him into Antioch and they began to teach the believers something they needed to know to be effective in reaching their city. Through this team of Barnabas and Saul, the Holy Spirit was setting the Antioch church in apostolic order. One of the dominate signs of true apostolic ministry is the ability to lay a spiritual foundation and build a structure that will handle a great outpouring of the Holy Spirit.

> "And God hath set some in the church, first apostles, secondarily prophets, thirdly teachers, after that miracles, then gifts of healings, helps, governments, diversities of tongues"
> (1 Corinthians 12:28 KJV).

Apostles are set in the church. Not just in the Antioch church described in the book of Acts, but in the churches of today as well. If there are still evangelists, pastors and teachers, then there are still apostles and prophets.

Governing Churches

If the New Testament church is to be effective and successful, then we must allow the Holy Spirit to set it in divine order. Today God is giving us an unfolding revelation of apostolic gifts along with an understanding of their function and operation. The most prominent gifts in the New Testament church were apostles and in the last days it will be the same.

Apostles are leadership gifts...

> given to the saints to equip them for the work of ministry

> set in the church to impart that which is lacking in training and governmental structure (Ephesians 4:12).

Many pastors are to blame for doing the work for the people. Where apostles are divinely called to break the co-dependency on the pastor and put a demand on the people to increase in maturity.

It's quite interesting that most religious denominations say that the apostolic office ended when John, last of the twelve apostles of the Lamb, died. Therefore, the very ministry gift that God anointed to set the church in order has been denied for the past two thousand years as even being existent.

Searching For Apostolic Increase

At least twenty-one people in the New Testament are called apostles, they are...

The Twelve Apostles of the Lamb

Matthias (Acts 1:26)

Barnabas and Paul (Acts 14:14)

Andronicus and Junius (Romans 16:7)

James our Lord's brother (Galations 1:19)

Epaphroditus (Philippians 2:25)

Silvanus and Timothy (1 Thessalonians 1:1, 2:6).

The word apostle, *apostolos,* appears some 80 times in the New Testament and *apostole,* apostleship, 4 times. The word apostle is from the Greek *apostolos,* meaning the one who is sent forth.

The apostle, being a sent one as a messenger, is derived from the Greek word *apo-stello.* Two Greek root words *apo* and *stello* make up the English word messenger.

Stello means to be dispatched on an expedition as one who has been commissioned and sent out on a journey.

Whereas *apo* means to be "sent out of and away from."

So then *apo-stello* (messenger) means to be sent forth, out of, away from, and on some sort of mission, thus, an ambassador, a delegate, a sent one. I believe that *apo*, the place that the messenger is sent out from is, in fact, the local church and we will discuss this in greater detail in Chapter Eight.

SAUL'S
DAYS OF PREPARATION

But where had Saul been before Antioch? He had been receiving revelation, teaching and training from the Holy Spirit. There are always times of preparation in the lives of every believer. Times when we are hidden in the desert places of life only to be launched out at the proper time (Luke 1:80). The total transformation of a person is one of the greatest miracles of God.

Saul was being made ready for such a time as this. Indeed the heart of the Spirit of God is to lead us all to a place of understanding that his mighty power is extended to those who believe. The word declares, "the eyes of your understanding being enlightened; that ye may know what is the hope of his calling, and what the riches of the glory of his inheritance in the saints, {19} And what is the exceeding greatness of his power to us-ward who believe, according to the working of his mighty power" (Ephesians 1:18-19 KJV).

Our Lord called Saul to follow him, not because of what he was in himself, but because of what he would become under the Holy Spirit's guidance. "To whom God would make known what is the riches of the glory of this mystery among the Gentiles; which is Christ in you, the hope of glory" (Colossians 1:27 KJV).

LITTLE ANOINTED ONES

The disciples were first called Christians in Antioch. Before that, they were oftentimes referred to as the *way:*

> "If he found any of this *way*" (Acts 9:2, 16:17).

> "There was no small stir about that *way*" (Acts 19:23).

> Jesus spoke of himself as the *Way* (John 14:6).

Any reference to the *way* was soon eclipsed by a new name, Christian. The Bible provides a definition of disciples: "If you abide in me, and my words abide in you, you shall ask what you will, and it shall be done unto you. Herein is my Father glorified, that you bear much fruit; so shall you be my disciples" (John 15:7-8 KJV).

Antioch was known as a city that coined new words and phrases. I believe the name Christian came from Paul's teaching the Gentile believers in Antioch about the Christ.

The word Christ literally means, "Messiah or The Anointed One." The disciples were often referred to as "Christ-ones" in Antioch. Why? Because of the demonstration of signs, wonders, and miracles seen at the hands of these believers who were doing and not just hearing, "He that believeth on me, the works that I do shall he do also; and greater works than these shall he do; because I go unto my Father" (John 14:12).

Watchman Nee has some very interesting comments on the Antioch church.

> "The church in Antioch is the model church shown us in God's Word because it was the first to come into being after the founding of the churches connected with the Jews and the Gentiles. In Acts chapter two we see the church in

connection with the Jews established in Jerusalem, and in chapter ten we see the church in connection with the Gentiles established in the house of Cornelius. It was just after the establishment of these churches that the church in Antioch from the very outset stood on absolutely clear church ground. It is of no little significance that the disciples were first called Christians in Antioch (Acts 11:26). It was there that the peculiar characteristics of the Christian and the Christian church were first clearly manifested, for this reason it may be regarded as the pattern church for this dispensation."
Watchman Nee
The Normal Christian Church Life
1980 Living Stream Ministry, Anaheim, Ca.

So from the acts of these doing believers on the streets of Antioch came a coined phrase that would last throughout eternity, Christians -- little anointed ones! The name Christian came about because of the demonstration of the anointing and apostolic grace on the Antioch believers.

A RESURRECTED JESUS

Many of those who follow other religions in the world must see the power of God in demonstration before we can capture their attention long enough for conviction to take hold. When we leave the Christian cultures of the world and minister in other cultures, in order to produce results, the people must experience a resurrected Jesus.

God's calling card to an unbelieving world are signs, wonders, and miracles. The responsibility of reaching the world for Jesus does not belong to a few chosen ones, but in fact has been placed on the church as a whole.

The people in Antioch believed in a resurrected Jesus because they saw the believers preaching on the streets with resurrection power.

Let's see some examples.

> The people of Samaria believed the gospel after seeing signs and wonders (Acts 8:5-8).

> The multitudes followed Jesus, not only because of his great preaching ability, but because they were seeing and receiving miracles (John 6:2).

Searching For Apostolic Increase

"For our gospel did not come to you in word only, but also in power, and in the Holy Ghost, and in much assurance ..." (1 Thessalonians 1:5).

"But if I cast out demons with the finger of God, surely the kingdom of God has come upon you (Luke 11:20).

To summarize, the instruments of revival, awakening, and reaching the lost will all come about with the restoration of an apostolic church, filled with those endued with believing power and showing forth the excellencies of God (2 Corinthians 4:7). In an Antioch type of governing church the Holy Spirit releases *all* believers into ministry.

In the next chapter we will look at one of the strongest oppositions to the Antioch anointing -- the religious spirit.

SUMMARY: SEARCHING FOR APOSTOLIC INCREASE

☐ Apostolic gifts are spiritual pioneers who, through faith, are willing to press into the unknown and the unfamiliar.

☐ Apostolic leaders are champions of cooperation and not competition.

☐ The Greek word *(anazeteo)* indicates that it was not easy for Barnabas to find Saul. (Acts 11:25)

☐ Being obedient to follow the leading of the Holy Spirit requires the use of much diligence *(anazeteo)* in one's pursuit to lay hold onto a spiritual mantel.

☐ Today God is giving us an unfolding revelation of apostolic office gifts and function.

☐ Apostles are given to the saints to equip them for work. They are set to impart that which is lacking in training and governmental structure. (Ephesians 4:12)

☐ There are times of preparation in the lives of every believer, when we are hidden in the desert places of life only to be revealed at the proper time (Luke 1:80).

☐ From the acts of the doing believers in the streets of Antioch came a coined phrase that will last throughout eternity, Christians -- little anointed ones!

Governing Churches

CHAPTER 6
APOSTLES &
THE RELIGIOUS
CHURCH

Religion has a caretaker mentality with a don't-rock-the-boat mindset. It is cold, quiet, and formal. Where the pastor has been selected by some pulpit committee based on his religious education, affiliation or degrees.

One of the most deadly spiritual assignments against the church's ability to advance the gospel throughout the world is the religious spirit. I believe this spirit to be a murdering influence that is antichrist in nature and will be exposed by the Holy Spirit in these last days like never before. Thousands of good people have been taken captive and made ineffective by this spirit's deceptive influence.

In our society today, we have a dangerously false perception of church and many of the dynamics surrounding it. Through the years, we have come into a religious understanding of what a ministry and church is. Because of a false perception, the existing church will be powerfully challenged in the days to come by the reforming voice and ministry of the emerging apostles and prophets.

Before we get into the operations of the apostolic church, let's briefly examine the religious church and some of the religious paradigms to see if we can capture the spirit of religion in print.

THE RELIGIOUS CHURCH

The religious church is where people may get born again, gain their salvation ticket, then live out their lives unchallenged, unchanged, and just waiting to die. This is the church where one can listen to a nice ten minute teaching or reading of a prayer and make apologies for not dismissing promptly at noon. A church that sends people back into a secular world with no spiritual impartation. This is the church who, during Sunday morning service, acknowledges everyone's birthdays, anniversaries and repents if they forgot one. This is the church where more emphasis is put on homecoming, fish fry's, bake sales and chicken dinners, rather than on what saith the Spirit of the Lord. Where the pastor is hard pressed to stand at the door after each service to kiss

Apostles & The Religious Church

babies and shake everyone's hand. This is the church where the pastor is pressured to piously visit all the people each week and make sure he is everybody's best friend. It is the place where one attends church only four times in their lifetime, to be dedicated, baptized, married and buried. It is full of programs run by businessmen, Type A personalities, controlling Jezebels and entertained by the occasional Sunday morning and Christmas cantatas. It is a place where one can fulfill comfortably their religious obligations. It has a caretaker mentality with a don't-rock-the-boat mindset. It is cold, quiet, and formal. Where the pastor has been selected by a pulpit committee based on his religious education, affiliation or degrees. Whose office walls are filled with plaques of men's recognition confirming that they had made the right choice.

In this church, the leadership is hired by people to do what they think is fitting rather than a man who was sent forth by the Holy Ghost. This is the church where the pastor is abused for twenty years and retired with a gold watch for faithful service, then sent off to some trailer park to die, only to repeat the same twenty-year pattern over again with someone else.

Governing Churches

This is the church where you can have two lives, a religious one and a secular one. This is the 'bless me only, but don't ask me to change, become involved, grow, mature, advance, pursue, increase, or do anything' church. It is full of those with spiritual religious sayings, flattery, smooth talkers and vain words, but themselves are not stable. This is the watching, griping, grumbling, whining church. This is the church where sin is seldom addressed and a false love just seems to cover even the unrepentant, rebellious and defiant.

In this church believers attend with the mind-set of being trained in ministry so that they might be equipped to do their own thing. This is the church where one can do according to his own heart with no accountability or submission to any leadership. In this church the preacher whips you and beats you with the word. This is the church that is intimidated by the grace and anointing on your life. Where people are bound because there is only room for the one man show. This is the church where thousands have soul ties because some relative once was a faithful member. This is the church that provides, with each membership, a place for the member and family to be buried in the church's cemetery. This is the church that builds tombs (Matthew 23:29).

Apostles & The Religious Church

The Word of God is quite clear about our relationship with this religious church. "Having a form of godliness, but denying the power thereof: from such turn away" (2 Timothy 3:5 KJV).

THE APOSTOLIC ANOINTING WILL CHALLENGE THE DURABILITY OF RELIGIOUS COMFORT ZONES.

After reading this short discourse you probably feel the same way that I do when I read it, terrible. If so, then we have captured and exposed the essence of the religious spirit. If your response however is anger, then I can only ask that you examine your heart before reading any further. Why? Because the apostolic anointing will challenge the durability of religious comfort zones.

Now we can turn away from religious bondage and enter the truly exciting world of apostolic ministry. In the next chapter we will look at the Antioch anointing's ability to tear down barriers and become a

multi-cultural, apostolic, breakthrough
ministry.

Apostles & The Religious Church

SUMMARY: APOSTLES & THE RELIGIOUS CHURCH

☐ One of the most deadly spiritual assignments against the church's ability to advance the gospel throughout the world is the religious spirit.

☐ The existing church will be powerfully challenged in the days to come by the reforming voice and ministry of the coming apostles.

☐ The Word of God is quite clear about our relationship with the religious spirit. "Having a form of godliness, but denying the power thereof: from such turn away" (2 Timothy 3:5 KJV).

☐ The apostolic anointing will challenge false religious belief systems that form error in the thinking of believers.

☐ Apostolic ministry gifts don't gather people simply to teach them truth, but rather to equip them for ministry.

☐ Apostolic gifts speak a fresh word as to what the Spirit of God is saying now whereas religious spirits dwell on what God hath said to the former move.

☐ Apostolic anointing ministers to the spirit of man where religious spirits speak to the head of man.

CHAPTER 7
APOSTOLIC CHURCHES OF ALL NATIONS

They came from all classes of society, from the wealthy and privileged to the street beggars, slaves and, yes, even criminals. They came from all manners of religious traditions, pagan sorcery, mystic cults, Greek mythology, idol worship and Judaism. Welcome to the apostolic church.

"Who shall not fear thee, O Lord, and glorify thy name? for thou only art holy: for all nations shall come and worship before thee; for thy judgments are made manifest" (Revelation 15:4 KJV).

The church in Antioch was a multi-national, multi-cultural church. Religious churches have an extreme difficulty transcending or breaking out of ministry from one culture only into another.

However, the church in Antioch was filled with those from various cultures and races. They came from all classes of

85

society, from the wealthy and privileged to the street beggars, slaves and, yes, even criminals. They came from all manner of religious traditions, pagan sorcery, mystic cults, Greek mythology, idol worship and Judaism. "Now there were in the church that was at Antioch certain prophets and teachers; as Barnabas, and Simeon that was called Niger, and Lucius of Cyrene, and Manaen, which had been brought up with Herod the tetrarch, and Saul" (Acts 13:1 KJV).

RELIGIOUS CHURCHES HAVE AN EXTREME DIFFICULTY TRANSCENDING OR BREAKING OUT OF MINISTRY FROM ONE CULTURE.

Scripture declares that there were prophets and teachers in the Antioch church. We have already described Barnabas, a Levite, who was known as the son of rest. Let's take a moment to look at the others named, who probably made up the governing presbytery of the Antioch church.

SIMEON CALLED NIGER

His name means hearkening. Niger means to be black. Simeon could very well be the same man, named Simon, that was the one who carried Jesus' cross on that wearisome Delerosa road to his crucifixion (Mark 15:21, Luke 23:26). He was called Simon of Cyrene (North Africa). He was the only one whom the blood of Jesus touched on the way to Calvary. Can you imagine that? "And as they came out, they found a man of Cyrene, Simon by name: him they compelled to bear his cross" (Matthew 27:32). So we discover that a black North African was one of the founding pillars, and prophets in the church at Antioch.

Today thousands of Africans are being launched out by the Holy Spirit all over the world as ambassadors of Christ. Some of the largest churches in Europe have, at the helm of leadership, black African apostles and prophets with hundreds of evangelists who are carrying God's glory throughout the cities.

LUCIUS OF CYRENE

There was also Lucius of Cyrene named in the church in Antioch. Lucius was a Gentile whose name means light. He was probably very prophetic and full of revelation. We also see him later being sent out on one of the Antioch apostolic teams (Romans 16:21).

MANAEN

Then there was Manaen. His name means comforter. He was raised as a foster brother of Herod the Tetrarch, the governor of Antipas and the ruler who killed John the Baptist. Manaen was a noted member of society and a well-educated man. We would relate to him today as a professional.

TO BE TRULY APOSTOLIC MEANS TO BE SENT FORTH, AND THIS IS THE FIRST IDENTIFYING MARK OF AN APOSTLE.

With the restoration of the apostolic anointing will come great witty inventions that will produce great wealth. Thousands of anointed business professionals are taking hold of the apostolic anointing and using all their resources to advance the gospel of Jesus Christ.

SAUL

Then of course Saul's name is mentioned. Saul (Paul) was also part of this Antioch apostolic church. He was a man raised in Judaism under the powerful teaching of Gamaliel. (Acts 22:3) He was well versed in the scriptures, had a divine encounter with Jesus, was a Hellenistic Jew from Tarsus and had the covenanted Roman citizenship. Apostolic churches have the ability to break out of one particular culture and religious system while uniting together under one cause -- His!

UNVEILING
THE APOSTOLIC CHURCH

What we see in Antioch was the formation of an apostolic team. "Now there were in the church that was at Antioch certain prophets and teachers; as Barnabas, and Simeon that was called Niger, and Lucius of Cyrene, and Manaen, which had been brought up with Herod the tetrarch, and Saul" (Acts 13:1 KJV).

At this point, we are about to discover the unveiling of the sending power of the first New Testament apostolic church. As this multi-cultural group of leaders gathered together in prayer and fasting, the Holy Ghost said, "Separate me Barnabas and Saul for the work that I have called them." Notice who was directing the church, the Holy Spirit. "As they ministered to the Lord, and fasted, the Holy Ghost said, Separate me Barnabas and Saul for the work whereunto I have called them. {3} And when they had fasted and prayed, and laid their hands on them, they sent them away" (Acts 13:2-3 KJV). Consider who is directing the church -- the Holy Spirit. It's time to be sent forth, apostolic!

APOSTOLIC PRESBYTERIES

Keep in mind that this group of leaders (presbytery) was made up of prophets and teachers (not pastors and evangelists). This same group prophesied and laid their hands on Barnabas and Saul.

An assembly of believers only become a local church when governmental elders have been set in place (Acts 14:23; Titus 1:4-5; Hebrews 13:7,17; 1 Thessalonians 5:12-13, 1 Peter 5:1-4). These elders make up a presbytery as seen here in the Antioch church.

The formation of a presbytery may not happen overnight. However, there is something special and quite powerful when we understand the power of an apostolic presbytery. I believe that there is much restoration of truth coming in this area to the body of Christ.

We often see in the scriptures where apostles and elders are assembled together (Acts 15:2,4,6,22,23; 16:4; 21:18). Timothy himself was confirmed into ministry by a presbytery. As the scripture reads, "Neglect not the gift that is in thee, which was given thee by prophecy, with the laying on of the hands of the presbytery" (1 Timothy 4:14 KJV).

WITH THE RESTORATION OF THE APOSTOLIC MINISTRY WILL COME THE REVELATION OF THE IMPORTANCE OF TEAM WORK.

APOLUO

"And when they had fasted and prayed, and laid their hands on them, they sent them away" (Acts 13:3 KJV). The Greek word for sent is *apoluo*. To be truly apostolic means to be sent forth, and this is the first identifying mark of an apostle.

Governing Churches

"Paul an apostle, not sent from men, nor through the agency of man, but through Jesus Christ, and God the Father, who raised Him from the dead ...." (Galations 1:1). It's important to see the maturity of the church in Antioch. It was from, or out of (*Greek: apo*), this church, through the ministry of a presbytery and the laying on of hands that the Holy Spirit separated and sent forth this apostolic team.

APOSTOLIC CHURCHES RELEASE THEIR LEADERS INTO THE HARVEST FIELDS OF THE NATIONS AND DO NOT TRY TO HOLD THEM BACK.

Apostolic anointing carries a burning passionate fervor that commands change. Their strong call is to strengthen, encourage, and motivate the church to action. Apostolic anointing commands advancement. The sending forth of these men, Barnabas and Saul, was not the pattern of men who simply decided to go out on their own. This was the development of an apostolic governing church that we could refer to as the gathering place of the sent ones.

Notice, too, the development of an apostolic team; this is not one saint who loves God doing his own thing. Jesus had already demonstrated the apostolic team pattern with the sending of the twelve and later the seventy (Matt 10:1, Luke 10:1). With the restoration of the apostolic ministry will come the revelation of the importance of team work.

Imagine the spiritual maturity and strength of this church to be able to send out two of its most distinguished leaders. Apostolic churches release their leaders into the harvest fields of the nations and do not try to hold them back.

FASTING AND PRAYER

Apostolic governing churches are fasting and praying churches. Among the strongest identifying graces on an apostolic church is its prayer life. They are fervent, militant and, yes, even loud. They understand that fervent prayer makes much of God's apostolic power available (James 5:16). Paul makes mention even of travailing in prayer (Galations 4:19, 1 Thessalonians 2:9, 2 Thessalonians 3:8).

The Antioch presbytery fasted and prayed, and then laid their hands on Barnabas and Saul. The prophets and teachers (presbytery), along with the church (the assembled called out ones, the Christians) had assembled themselves together to pray. It was then that the Holy Spirit decided it was time to launch out this church's first team of sent ones, the Antioch apostles.

Prayer is the breeding ground of ministry assignments.

They were now moving in the, *apostolos.* The structural model of the New Testament apostolic church was birthed through prayer in Antioch.

APOSTLES ARE SEPARATED BY THE HOLY SPIRIT, GIVEN APOSTOLIC AUTHORITY AND A TERRITORY OF SPIRITUAL JURISDICTION (METRON).

Note also that this church acknowledged the Holy Spirit as the supreme director and administrator of the church, and He had the liberty, through prophecy, to call and separate unto Himself an apostolic team.

Apostolic Churches Of All Nations

SPIRITUAL JURISDICTION

"As they ministered to the Lord, and fasted, the Holy Ghost said, *Separate* me Barnabas and Saul for the work whereunto I have called them" (Acts 13:2 KJV Italics added). The Greek word to separate is *aphorizo* meaning ...

to mark off from others

issue spiritual boundaries

This, therefore, is a separation *(aphorizo)* unto the Holy Spirit's direct supervision and leading while at the same time creating a territory and boundary of spiritual jurisdiction. Paul describes this boundary like this, "But we will not boast of things without our measure *(metron, i.e.,* place of spiritual authority and jurisdiction), but according to the measure of the rule which God hath distributed to us, a measure to reach even unto you" (2 Corinthians 10:13 KJV). Apostles are ...

separated by the Holy Spirit

given apostolic authority

given a territory of spiritual jurisdiction (*metron*)

95

It is in this territory or *metron* that the apostolic anointing functions at its highest level.

SENT, NEVER TO RETURN AGAIN, IS SELDOM, IF EVER, GOD'S APOSTOLIC PLAN.

SEPARATED AND NEVER SEEN AGAIN?

It is important to understand that in New Testament apostolic churches people are not trained and sent out to remain separated from the local church forever. There is a misconception of using churches for their ability to raise up people to pursue their own ministries. God forbid! Sent, never to return again, is seldom, if ever, God's apostolic plan.

Throughout Paul's ministry, he continued to return to his home church in Antioch rather than his hometown of Tarsus:

Apostolic Churches Of All Nations

Paul and Barnabas return to Antioch after their first apostolic journey (Acts 14:26-28).

Paul, Barnabas, along with John Mark, return to Antioch after attending the council in Jerusalem that addressed the issue of circumcision (Acts 15:30).

Paul, Timothy and Silas return to Antioch (Acts 15:40-18:22).

Paul surely would have returned again to Antioch had he not been detained and sent to Rome (Acts 23; 27:1; 28:16-17).

God uses apostolic ministry to train up believers who are sent out for seasons and specific works, however they return again to the local governing church for additional assignments. We must come to the place of understanding the value of the local church. Jesus said, "I will build my church and the gates of hell will not prevail" (Matthew 16:18). He never said that he would build your own, separate from a local church, ministry. Apostolic people must get the revelation of teamwork and the value of being a part of a local governing church.

APOSTOLIC PEOPLE MUST GET THE REVELATION OF TEAMWORK AND THE VALUE OF BEING A PART OF A LOCAL GOVERNING CHURCH.

When our Lord said the church, he did not say kingdom. Many people say they are a part of the kingdom or that they are the church wherever they go. This is tragic and I have never met anyone with lasting fruit that made such statements. We preach the kingdom, yes, but we build the church (Matthew 10:7; Luke 4:43, 9:2,60; Matthew 16.18). Get involved with a local, Holy Spirit-led, church that carries an apostolic anointing. Being part of a team in a local church is not a question of losing your identity, but rather of finding your place of effectiveness so that you might bring forth much fruit (John 15:16-19).

"To appoint unto them that mourn in Zion, to give unto them beauty for ashes, the oil of joy for mourning, the garment of praise for the spirit of heaviness; that they might be called trees of righteousness, the planting of the LORD, that he might be glorified" (Isaiah 61:3 KJV).

The leaders of apostolic churches are not some sort of elite clique. They recognize, probably more than any other ascension gift, that they cannot reach this world for Jesus alone. It is the heart pressed disposition of every apostolic ministry to help you find your place in the body of Christ. Every member is important and should be active in the work of ministry (Ephesians 4).

APOSTOLIC GIFTS ARE KNOWN FOR DRAWING AND RAISING UP LEADERS.

TIMES OF PREPARATION

A regular pattern for the preparation of God's team is the time of preparation in the wilderness. Most, reading this book, have passed through a wilderness place in their spiritual lives. Before God will send you forth (*apostolos*) he must prepare you for your future.

Governing Churches

God doesn't send forth just anyone, we must become disciples (learners) before we can possibly become teachers. Apostolic ministry is known for its stability and will not allow flakiness to survive unchallenged. An apostle...

teaches

trains

disciples

imparts spiritual strength

... into those who surround them. Apostolic gifts are known for drawing and raising up leaders.

Apostolic grit must be formed in a person so that they are able to handle the pressure of ministry and the spiritual warfare involved. *Reformation and revival never come without a battle.* This may have been the source of the sharp conflict between Paul and Barnabas when disputing over John Mark staying on the team (Acts 15:37-39). Perhaps Paul did not think that John Mark had the apostolic fortitude necessary to overcome the teams many obstacles because he had broken rank once before.

We must come into spiritual maturity with a solid Christian character which is vital to the success of our training (2 Peter 1:5-8). To be used of God you must...

forsake sin

be born again

renew your mind

study the word

become a doer of the word

commit yourself fully

plug in to a local church

get trained

become a part of God's apostolic church

Remember, times of preparation are not wasted times but cherished times.

FIVE EXAMPLES OF WILDERNESS PREPARATION

1. Moses moved ahead of the timing of the Lord and ended up killing an Egyptian because of a carnal zeal for God. He then spent

the next forty years in the backside of the desert, alone with sheep and looking at a mountain before he was ready to be sent as a deliverer (Exodus 3:1).

2. David, the anointed king of war, was hidden as a young lad in the wilderness being prepared to meet Goliath, the Philistine champion of fear (1 Samuel 17:34-35).

3. There was a tribe of men called the Gadites who fought with David. These were wilderness men of might who were fit, and made ready in the desert for battle. They had learned how to live in victory during wilderness times (1 Chronicles 12:8).

4. John the Baptist was hidden in the deserts until the time of his revealing unto Israel (Luke 1:80). He was a voice crying in the wilderness.

5. Jesus himself was led into the wilderness to be tempted of the devil for forty days and nights. Here we see Jesus repeatedly declaring, "Satan, it is written." Jesus is our supreme example of

passing through the wilderness,
but coming out with power to
shake the nations (Luke 4:1-13).

You too are being prepared for a day of
revealing, so don't run from the times of
preparation. Let the Holy Spirit do a
mighty work in you by submitting yourself
to a spiritual father. As the Apostle Paul
says so wonderfully, "For though ye have
ten thousand instructors in Christ, yet
have ye not many fathers: for in Christ
Jesus I have begotten you through the
gospel. {16} Wherefore I beseech you, be ye
followers of me" (1 Corinthians 4:15-16
KJV).

A GREAT NET

The Spirit of God is telling us that he is
building a great apostolic net for a great
catch. The strength of this net is
dependent upon the strength of our
relationships between one another. We
must recognize the importance of one
another in this hour. The strength of this
net will be the covenants between
apostolic leaders. The knots are prophetic
examples of the strength of this net.

Can you imagine a network (knots)
of ministry gifts stretched around

the world, in every city and in every nation?

Can you picture the strength of hundreds of thousands of networking apostolic churches with thousands of intercessors?

Can you see that we could mobilize thousands of teams to go into our cities and nations with the power of the gospel and the anointing to witness?

In the ensuing chapter we will take a look at the pioneering capacity of the sent ones.

Apostolic Churches Of All Nations

SUMMARY: APOSTOLIC CHURCHES OF ALL NATIONS

☐ Religious churches have extreme difficulty transcending or breaking out of ministry from one culture only into another.

☐ The Greek word sent is *apoluo*. To be truly apostolic means to be sent.

☐ Apostolic churches are fasting and praying churches.

☐ One of the strongest identifying graces on an apostolic church is its prayer life. They are fervent, militant and, yes, even loud.

☐ We have a misconception of using churches for their ability to raise us up to pursue our own ministries.

☐ Sent, never to return again, is seldom, if ever, God's apostolic plan.

☐ God uses apostolic ministry to train up believers who are sent out for seasons and specific works who

Governing Churches

will return again to the local
church for additional assignments.

CHAPTER 8
APOSTLES,
THE SENT ONES

Apostolic anointings are pioneering, go first, vanguard anointings. Apostolic people are trail blazers in the realm of the spirit. They are the go first, cutting-edge, gifts that many religious people are so uncomfortable with.

PIONEERS

We have read a lot about being apostolic. We know now that apostolic means to be sent forth by the Holy Spirit with a specific task. We also know that to be truly apostolic there must be a local church involved to be sent out from. This local church will carry an apostolic anointing that manifests in people carrying a strong desire to go into their local territories and even into the nations of the world. These would be the sent ones.

There is something incredibly powerful about being sent forth. More than any other ministry, apostolic anointings are pioneering, go first, vanguard anointings. Apostolic people are trail blazers in the realm of the spirit. They are the go first, cutting-edge, gifts that many religious people are so uncomfortable with.

TO BE SENT FORTH FROM A LOCAL CHURCH ON AN APOSTOLIC TEAM IS THE HIGHEST CALLING A SAINT CAN RECEIVE.

When the Holy Spirit sends you to the nations to minister, it should be out of a church with an Antioch type of release. Today, many people are roaming around the world trying to do something great for God, but are not a part of any local church. Again, Jesus said, "I will build my church and the gates of hell would not prevail." Ministry has a purpose, to build a local church (base, stronghold of God), advance the Holy Spirit's purpose in a particular territory and to be sent forth as part of a ministry team. To be sent forth from a local church on an apostolic team is the highest calling a saint can receive.

It carries with it the highest of anointings and purpose. A church that sends out apostolic teams into the harvest fields of the world is the highest manifestation of an apostolic church. Let's look at some more Biblical patterns of being sent forth *(apostolos)* ones.

JESUS WAS SENT

"But when the fullness of the time was come, *God sent forth his Son,* made of a woman, made under the law, {5} To redeem them that were under the law, that we might receive the adoption of sons. {6} And because ye are sons, God hath sent forth the Spirit of his Son into your hearts, crying, Abba, Father. {7} Wherefore thou art no more a servant, but a son; and if a son, then an heir of God through Christ" (Galations 4:4-7 KJV Italics added).

JOHN THE BAPTIST WAS SENT

"Behold, I will *send* you Elijah the prophet before the coming of the great and dreadful day of the LORD" (Malachi 4:5 KJV Italics added).

THE HOLY GHOST WAS SENT

"But when the Comforter is come, whom *I will send* unto you from the Father, even the Spirit of truth, which proceedeth from the Father, he shall testify of me" (John 15:26 KJV Italics added).

THE TWELVE APOSTLES WERE SENT

"And when he had called unto him his twelve disciples, he gave them power against unclean spirits, to cast them out, and to heal all manner of sickness and all manner of disease. {2} Now the names of the twelve apostles are these; The first, Simon, who is called Peter, and Andrew his brother; James the son of Zebedee, and John his brother; {3} Philip, and Bartholomew; Thomas, and Matthew the publican; James the son of Alphaeus, and Lebbaeus, whose surname was Thaddaeus; {4} Simon the Canaanite, and Judas Iscariot, who also betrayed him. {5} These twelve Jesus *sent forth*, and commanded them, saying, Go not into the way of the Gentiles, and into any city of the Samaritans enter ye not: {6} But go rather to the lost sheep of the house of Israel. {7} And as ye go, preach, saying, The kingdom of heaven is at hand. {8} Heal the sick, cleanse the lepers, raise the dead, cast out devils: freely ye have received, freely give" (Matthew 10:1-8 KJV Italics added).

THE SEVENTY WERE SENT

"After these things the Lord appointed other seventy also, and *sent them* two and two before his face into every city and place, whither he himself would come" (Luke 10:1 KJV Italics added).

MODERN APOSTLES ARE SENT ONES

"And how shall they preach, except they *be sent?* as it is written, How beautiful are the feet of them that preach the gospel of peace, and bring glad tidings of good things!" (Rom 10:15 KJV Italics added).

Those that are sent have the power and authority of those who have sent them.

YOU ARE SENT

And finally, you are sent! "*Go ye into all the world and preach the gospel to every creature*" (Mark 16:15 KJV Italics added).

Being sent *(apostello)* is the most powerful manifestation of an apostolic governmental anointing. "As thou hast sent *(apostello)* me into the world, even so have I also sent *(apostello)* them into the world "(John 17:18 KJV). This apostolic structure of being sent forth from a local church will challenge many in our generation who are doing their own thing under the guise that the Holy Spirit is leading them.

People often call our church asking me if they can come in and minister to the saints at Spirit of Life Ministries. Usually, I ask them these questions:

Who are you?

Where are you planted?

Who is sending you?

What do you have?

Apostles The Sent Ones

Why do I ask them? Because I am looking for sent ones, not went ones. Loving Jesus alone is not enough. You must be a builder of the church.

Apostolic churches are networking together with sent ones and not with lone ranger types. This apostolic way will directly challenge the religious thinking of today but it will help bring stability to a flaky generation that has been disarmed by religious tradition and soulish ambitions. The glorious church will be filled with thousands of apostolic teams, not saints wondering around doing their own thing, but anointed builders who are sent out on assignments from local churches.

Next we will spend some time looking at the territorial opposition against apostolic ministry.

Governing Churches

SUMMARY: APOSTLES, THE SENT ONES

☐ Apostolic anointings are pioneering, go first, vanguard anointings.

☐ To be apostolically sent out from a local church is the highest calling a saint can receive.

☐ To be a church that sends out apostolic teams into the harvest fields of the world is the highest manifestation of an apostolic church.

☐ Apostolic churches are networking together with sent ones and not with lone ranger types.

CHAPTER 9
APOSTLES & TERRITORIAL OPPOSITION

Apostolic ministry is strategic, with purpose and design and will impact gateway cities with teams that have been prepared to meet the demonic representatives of territories.

IMPACTING GATEWAY CITIES

After being sent forth from the local church in about 45 AD by the Holy Ghost, Barnabas and Saul departed on their apostolic (sent) journey. They were now fully apostolic and being sent forth by the Holy Spirit himself. John Mark accompanied them. "And when they were at Salamis, they preached the word of God in the synagogues of the Jews: and they had also John to their minister" (Acts 13:5 KJV).

This is probably the same John Mark who would later author the second gospel. His mother Mary was a woman of prominence in Jerusalem, where many

115

saints gathered together during Peter's imprisonment under Herod Agrippa (Acts 12:12).

Barnabas and Paul took John Mark with them to Antioch as part of their team after delivering a famine relief offering to the church in Jerusalem. John's function on the team was that of minister or assistant to the needs of the team, and probably included:

intercession

making of travel arrangements

food and lodging plans

and perhaps some teaching

This was a time of training and ministry development for him.

After being sent forth (*apostolos*) by the Holy Ghost from the apostolic church in Antioch, Barnabas, Paul and John Mark were launched out on what is commonly referred to as Paul's first missionary journey. However, in reality, this is the first apostolic mission or assignment from the Antioch church and these men were the Antioch apostles, they were a team.

Earlier, the spread of the gospel had been the result of persecution, but now we see the manifestation of a truly apostolic design. Apostolic ministry is strategic with purpose and design, and will impact gateway cities.

APOSTOLIC TEAMS MUST BE PREPARED TO MEET THE DEMONIC REPRESENTATIVES OF TERRITORIES.

Today, half of the population of the world is gathered in gateway cities. (See appendix one). Gateway cities or territories are recognized not only by large population, but by their importance to the nation as well. This importance can be measured in many ways, including:

commerce

travel

historical significance

cultural and musical influence

education

As the Spirit of God continues with the restoration of the apostolic church, the

117

ability to identify and better understand gateway cities and territories will increase. We can expect the Holy Spirit to establish Antioch type governing churches in these places.

Apostles are architects and master builders in the realm of the spirit. This team of Antioch apostles traveled inland to the seacoast town of Seleucia then sailed on to Cyprus, Barnabas' home (Acts 4:36). Cyprus was the bridge for international travel, and was a spiritual hub and the home base of Barnabas' operations later in his ministry (Acts 11:19-20, 15:36-39).

FALSE SPIRITUAL GOVERNMENT IS DEMONICALLY SET IN TERRITORIES TO CONTROL AND INFLUENCE LEADERSHIP.

At Salamis, the team preached the word of God in the synagogues to the Jews first. The team established something here that they did on a regular basics; preach to the Jews first, but not exclusively (Romans 1:16). This would be impractical for us today, and Paul later changed his method

118

as well. "Then Paul and Barnabas waxed bold, and said, It was necessary that the word of God should first have been spoken to you: but seeing ye put it from you, and judge yourselves unworthy of everlasting life, lo, we turn to the Gentiles. {47} For so hath the Lord commanded us, saying, I have set thee to be a light of the Gentiles, that thou shouldest be for salvation unto the ends of the earth" (Acts 13:46 KJV).

Even though Paul and Barnabas ceased taking the gospel to the Jew first does not imply that we should restrict evangelism to Gentiles. We must have a heart to reach Jews with the saving gospel of our Jewish Messiah Jesus.

"So they, being sent forth by the Holy Ghost, departed unto Seleucia; and from thence they sailed to Cyprus. {5} And when they were at Salamis, they preached the word of God in the synagogues of the Jews: and they had also John to their minister" (Acts 13:4-5 KJV).

OCCULT OPPOSITION

As the team traveled through the isle of Cyprus unto the town of Paphos, the capital city of Cyprus, they met Bar-Jesus (son of salvation). This man was a...

sorcerer (magician)

false prophet

Jew

Paphos was the site of a famous temple to the Goddess Astarte, the goddess of Jezebel. False apostles, religious spirits, and the spirit of Jezebel will be the three main powers of opposition to the apostolic church in the last days. Apostolic teams must be prepared to meet the demonic representatives of territories.

Since they are the sent ones, they have the grace and anointing on their lives that cause these dark territorial governors to manifest. Apostles are not peacemakers when it comes to spiritual opposition. Apostolic teams are sent by God as divine instruments used to challenge these demonic spiritual strongholds so that God can establish what he has started. *The objective of spiritual warfare is to remove the hindrances to the gospel.* "And when they had gone through the isle unto Paphos, they found a certain sorcerer, a false prophet, a Jew, whose name was Barjesus" (Acts 13:6 KJV). False spiritual government is demonically set in territories to control and influence leadership.

APOSTLES ARE NOT PEACE MAKERS WHEN IT COMES TO SPIRITUAL OPPOSITION.

Territorial governors seek out positions of power and influence. This false prophet, Bar-Jesus, was standing guard over Sergius Paulus, the Roman ruler of the island of Cyprus. Apostolic churches are called to influence their territories and are divinely equipped to hit Satan hard and make him move.

PHILIP'S OPPOSITION IN SAMARIA

When Philip preached in Samaria his first opposition was also a sorcerer. "But there was a certain man, called Simon, which beforetime in the same city used sorcery, and bewitched the people of Samaria, giving out that himself was some great one: {10} To whom they all gave heed, from the least to the greatest, saying, This man is the great power of God. {11} And to him they had regard, because that of long time he had bewitched them with sorceries" (Acts 8:9-11 KJV).

Governing Churches

"Now when the apostles which were at Jerusalem heard that Samaria had received the word of God, they sent unto them Peter and John: {15} Who, when they were come down, prayed for them, that they might receive the Holy Ghost: {16} (For as yet he was fallen upon none of them: only they were baptized in the name of the Lord Jesus.) {17} Then laid they their hands on them, and they received the Holy Ghost. {18} And when Simon saw that through laying on of the apostles' hands the Holy Ghost was given, he offered them money, {19} Saying, Give me also this power, that on whomsoever I lay hands, he may receive the Holy Ghost" (Acts 8:14-19 KJV).

Simon was a false prophet who had attached himself to Philip's ministry. It's common for evangelists and others to have people with soulish ambitions latch on to their ministries. Simon's heart was not right and it was exposed in the presence of the apostolic team of Peter and John.

Apostolic teams are called by God to confront these territorial guards. Right now in many parts of the world false personal prophecy given by spirits of divination is causing confusion in the body of Christ, attempting to undermine the true prophetic gifting (1 Corinthians 14:39). The restoration of the apostolic church will bring with it fearless men who will not tolerate these demonic spirits.

A GOVERNMENTAL STANDOFF

On the isle of Paphos, Sergius Paulus called for Barnabas and Saul because he desired to hear the word of God. Apostolic ministry teams are sent into gateway territories to open a way for the gospel.

"Which was with the deputy of the country, Sergius Paulus, a prudent man; who called for Barnabas and Saul, and desired to hear the word of God" (Acts 13:7 KJV).

Elymas' desire was to *withstand* this apostolic team. His demonic mandate was to *turn* the deputy away from the faith. "But Elymas the sorcerer (for so is his name by interpretation) withstood them, seeking to turn away the deputy from the faith" (Acts 13:8 KJV). The Greek word withstood is *anthistemi,* which means to set one's self against, to withstand, resist, or to intensely oppose. This shows us two parts of Elymas' demonic objectives:

to oppose God's ministers

to turn the hearts of the hearers

Governing Churches

Facing each other in fierce opposition are God's governmental apostolic team and Satan's territorial representative; governing authority verses governing authority. Elymas made it his business to stand against Barnabas and Saul just as the magicians in Pharaoh's court withstood Moses and Aaron.

Elymas set himself up as a voice from heaven in order to deceive the people. He was certainly a voice, but it was demonic. Just as Jannes and Jambres withstood Moses, Elymas severely opposed God's apostolic team. "Now as Jannes and Jambres withstood Moses, so do these also resist the truth: men of corrupt minds, reprobate concerning the faith" (2 Timothy 3:8 KJV).

THE UNSEEN BATTLES

Scripture makes it clear that there is an unseen battle raging in the spirit realm for the souls of man. Apostolic teams are God's battle ax to reach a lost and dying world (Jeremiah 51:20). Apostolic teams are called to...

open up new dimensions of worship and prayer

claim new territories for God

restore forgotten truth

preach sound doctrine

ignite   greater   operations   of
spiritual   gifts   when   needed
(Romans 1:11)

spearhead gospel operations

be spiritually equipped for battle

Apostolic leaders are not ignorant of the devil's devices and have been gifted to see beyond the natural and peer into the spiritual. "For we wrestle not against flesh and blood, but against principalities, against powers, against the rulers of the darkness of this world, against spiritual wickedness in high places" (Ephesians 6:12 KJV).

Then Saul, filled with the Holy Ghost, set his eyes on Elymas. Saul is not trying to be a nice statesman for Jesus, so he doesn't pull any punches with this false prophet. He calls Elymas a child of the devil and an enemy of righteousness. This is Holy Ghost boldness and authority in apostolic operation. "Then Saul, (who also is called Paul,) filled with the Holy Ghost, set his eyes on him, {10} And said, O full of all subtlety and all mischief, thou child of the devil, thou enemy of all righteousness, wilt thou not cease to pervert the right ways of the Lord? {11} And now, behold, the hand of the Lord is upon thee, and thou shalt be blind, not seeing the sun for a season. And immediately there fell on him a mist and a darkness; and he went about seeking some to lead him by the hand" (Acts 13:9-11 KJV).

APOSTOLIC MINISTRY TEAMS ARE SENT INTO GATEWAY TERRITORIES TO OPEN A WAY FOR THE GOSPEL.

Here we see the demonstration of the Spirit of God who himself had sent forth Barnabas and Saul to battle. Demonic government cannot stand against the purpose, power, and plan of God.

Paul set his eyes on Elymas, the false prophet. The Greek word for to set is *atenizo*, which means to look steadfastly; it is taken from the Greek root word *teino* meaning to stretch.

Paul, by the anointing on his life and the will of God, is literally locking onto and targeting Elymas, resulting in temporary blindness for this false prophet. Paul later declares, "And my speech and my preaching was not with enticing words of man's wisdom, but in demonstration of the Spirit and of power: {5} That your faith should not stand in the wisdom of men, but in the power of God" (1 Corinthians 2:4-5 KJV). We can always stand fearless in spiritual battle as the scripture declares, "And they went forth, and preached every where, the Lord working with them, and confirming the word with signs following" (Mark 16:20 KJV).

APOSTOLIC LEADERS ARE GRACED WITH THE ABILITY TO RECRUIT EVEN THE UNBELIEVER'S HELP.

The Roman deputy Paulus saw God's apostolic power in demonstration and believed, being astonished at the doctrine of the Lord. It wasn't just a power demonstration, it was the doctrine, or sound teaching about Jesus that turned this ruler's once deceived heart to our Lord. The Antioch apostolic team made such an impact on Paulus' life that history tells us that two generations of the descendants of Sergius Paulus served the

Lord Jesus Christ. Apostolic teams bring forth lasting fruit and their ministries affect future generations.

"Then the deputy, when he saw what was done, believed, being astonished at the doctrine of the Lord" (Acts 13:12 KJV).

MINISTERING TO TERRITORIAL LEADERS

Apostolic teams will meet those in governmental places of authority and minister to them. I have learned, through the years, as Ambassadors of Christ we should make an attempt to meet with those of authority. The ministry of an apostolic team will open up new realms in the spirit, encourage, bless, and will carry a refreshing and prophetic voice.

One year we took a team of people into rural Nicaragua where there had been reports of bandits and highway robbers. Upon arriving in the area we made three important stops.

Stop #1 Exploring the land
Because of the rural setting, it was necessary to explore the meeting site near the jungle village where the crusade meetings and the daily leadership training sessions would be held. We also needed to

see where meals for the team would be prepared.

Stop #2 Ministering to the local official in charge

We visited with the captain of the police in the area, letting him know why we were in the area and invited him and his family to join us. We had just stopped along the roadside where we picked up some food so we gave him a gift of piping hot tamales topped with some traditional goat cheese.

Stop #3 Ministering to the political leaders in charge

Finally, we went to meet with the village elder who also served as the mayor of the area. He was out of town on business, so we met with his wife at their hardware and grocery store. We brought them a gift, prayed for her and the family and blessed their business.

After these important stops, we had the cooperation of the secular leaders in the area. The night of our crusade, the police helped keep us safe by patrolling the outskirts of the area. They had become part of our apostolic team and through our efforts, many were born again to the glory of God. Apostolic leaders are graced with the ability to recruit even the unbeliever's help.

Governing Churches

The Holy Spirit is preparing the church for the powerful release of an apostolic company. In the following pages, we'll examine your place in this restoration.

Apostles And Territorial Opposition

☐ One of the marks of apostolic ministry is their spiritual understanding of the boundaries of their assigned territories (2 Corinthians 10:13-18).

☐ Apostolic ministry is strategic with purpose, design, and impacts gateway cities.

☐ Apostolic teams must be prepared to meet the demonic representatives of territorial authority.

☐ False spiritual government is demonically set in territories to control and influence leadership.

☐ Apostolic teams are God's battle ax to reach a lost and dying world. They are called to open up new dimensions of worship, prayer, and will ignite greater operations of spiritual gifts.

☐A truly apostolic team will meet those in governmental places of authority and minister to them.

Governing Churches

☐ Apostolic teams know how to recruit even the unbeliever's help.

CHAPTER 10
THE APOSTOLIC COMPANY

Before we see the manifestation of the glorious church, we will have a structural change take place enabling us to reach our cities. That structural change will release apostolic companies.

U nder our current method of having "church" we do everything we can to draw people to our buildings for services. The problem with that is, we end up shuffling religious people, who may already be believers, from one church to the next. Unfortunately, we still have not come into the understanding of going out and compelling the unchurched and unbelievers to come into God's house. Jesus said, "go out into the highways and hedges, and compel them to come in, that my house may be filled" (Luke 14:23 KJV).

A VISION FOR TEAMS

If we are going to see the manifestation of the glorious church (Ephesians 5:27) then we obviously need to have some sort

133

of structural change in the way we reach our cities. Apostolic ministry gifts bring structure and order to the church (Titus 1:5). We cannot expect change by doing the same old thing this year that did not work the year before.

Apostolic strategies are needed to reach our territories. Having apostolic teams sent out from Antioch type churches is one of those great strategies, and I believe many other strategies will be revealed to us through prayer as well. Instead of expecting the lost to come in on their own we must go out and get them.

BEING TEACHABLE IS ONE OF THE MAIN REQUIREMENTS OF AN APOSTOLIC TEAM MEMBER.

In Fort Lauderdale Florida, the territory at Spirit of Life Ministries, we have a population of approximately 1.4 million people in our county with only some 40,000 who attend church on Sunday morning (excluding Catholics).

Recently, we sent out two teams into a local harvest field in our territory. The teams' efforts resulted in nearly one hundred people being born again. At that rate, we could see twelve hundred souls saved by the year's end with just two teams! What if we had 20 teams laboring in the city? Then it would be conceivable to see 12,000 people born again by the year's end! How about 40 teams laboring in the city? Or 100 teams? Get the point? How awesome it would be to have bands of apostolic sent ones with character and purpose invading our cities!

APOSTLES NEVER IGNORE THE SPIRITUAL CONDITION OF THEIR TEAM.

EPHESUS PATTERN

Though we are moving closer to the understanding of the extreme need for apostolic teams, we must be fully aware that there are qualifications that team members must meet. Let's examine the apostolic pattern of ministry in Ephesus and the development of a team.

Paul is now a man of maturity and has learned much since his days in Antioch. We'll see how he takes what he learned and applies it to his territorial entrance and birthing of another signature apostolic ministry in Ephesus.

Chapter nineteen of the book of Acts is a fantastic example of apostolic leadership and the building of a team.

> "And it came to pass, that, while Apollos was at Corinth, Paul having passed through the upper coasts came to Ephesus: and finding certain disciples, {2} He said unto them, Have ye received the Holy Ghost since ye believed? And they said unto him, We have not so much as heard whether there be any Holy Ghost. {3} And he said unto them, Unto what then were ye baptized? And they said, Unto John's baptism. {4} Then said Paul, John verily baptized with the baptism of repentance, saying unto the people, that they should believe on him which should come after him, that is, on Christ Jesus. {5} When they heard this, they were baptized in the name of the Lord Jesus" (Acts 19:1-5 KJV).

KEY ONE: COMMITTED DISCIPLES

This Scripture illustrates how the apostle Paul demonstrated his understanding of apostolic ministry; he put first things first by gathering disciples.

The Bible states that a requirement for apostolic teams is discipleship. A disciple (*mathetes*) is one who abides and lives in God's word (John 8:31). Disciples of Christ are lifelong students of the word of God. "Study to show thyself approved unto God, a workman that needeth not to be ashamed, rightly dividing the word of truth" (2 Timothy 2:15 KJV). Disciples long for solid doctrine, and are not only students of the word, but are also teachable. Being teachable is one of the main requirements of an apostolic team member.

Apostolic people are Word people, but they are doers of the Word, not hearers only (James 1:22). There are many believers, but few disciples.

Apostles have the anointing necessary to pull together disciples and put them to work as a team. Notice that Paul first asked them if they had received the Holy Ghost since they believed. Their response was that they had never heard about the

Holy Ghost. "And when Paul had laid his hands upon them, the Holy Ghost came on them; and they spake with tongues, and prophesied" (Acts 19:6 KJV).

Paul understood the utter importance of his team being filled with Holy Ghost power, and knew what Jesus meant when he said, "But you shall receive power *after* that the Holy Ghost is come upon you: and you shall be witnesses unto me..." (Acts 1:8). Notice he says, *after* and not before. Apostles never ignore the spiritual condition of their team.

KEY TWO:
FILLED
WITH THE HOLY GHOST

Apostolic teams must be filled with the Holy Ghost to be effective in ministry. There is no way to handle the extreme pressure and opposition to the gospel without the free gift of Jesus' *dumanis* power to witness, the Holy Spirit himself.

BAPTISM OF
THE HOLY SPIRIT

After Jesus' resurrection, he commanded his disciples not to depart from Jerusalem, but to wait for the promise of the Father. Jesus had spoken of this same promise when he said, "If you love me, keep my commandments. And I will pray the Father, and he shall give you another Comforter, that he may abide with you forever, even the Spirit of truth; whom the world cannot receive, because it seeth him not, neither knoweth him: but you know him; for he dwelleth with you, and shall be in you" (John 14:15-17). Jesus declared, "For John truly baptized with water; but you shall be baptized with the Holy Ghost not many days hence." Jesus also told them that they would "receive power after that the Holy Ghost was come upon them and that they would be witnesses unto him" (Acts 1:4-8).

APOSTOLIC MANTLES RELEASE THE GIFTS OF THE SPIRIT.

John the Baptist also prophesied of this great event saying, "I indeed baptize you with water unto repentance: but he that cometh after me is mightier than I, whose shoes I am not worthy to bear: he shall baptize you with the Holy Ghost and with fire" (Matthew 3:11).

Governing Churches

Then that precious day came. "And when the day of Pentecost was fully come, they were all with one accord in one place, and suddenly there came a sound from heaven as of a rushing mighty wind, and it filled all the house where they were sitting. And there appeared unto them cloven tongues like as of fire, and it sat upon each of them. And they were all filled with the Holy Ghost, and began to speak with other tongues, as the Spirit gave them utterance" (Acts 2:1-4).

The Apostle Peter was in the upper room that day and was himself filled with this Holy Ghost power and spoke with other tongues. After he left the building people asked him the same question that is being asked today, "What meaneth this?" After Peter heard that question he spoke his first Holy Ghost empowered sermon. His message pierced the hearts of the hearers and they asked, "What shall we do?" The same Peter that had just days before denied the Lord Jesus responded with a great boldness saying, "Repent, and be baptized everyone of you in the name of Jesus Christ for the remission of sins, and you shall receive the gift of the Holy Ghost. For the promise is unto you, and to your children, and to all that are afar off, even as many as the Lord our God shall call" (Acts 2:37-39).

The Apostolic Company

When Paul came across the believers in Ephesus, he asked them this question, "Have you received the Holy Ghost since you believed? And they said unto him, We have not so much as heard whether there be any Holy Ghost. And he said unto them, Unto what then were you baptized? And they said, Unto John's baptism. Then said Paul, John verily baptized with the baptism of repentance, saying unto the people, that they should believe on him which should come after him, that is, on Christ Jesus. When they heard this, they were baptized in the name of the Lord Jesus. And when Paul had laid his hands upon them, the Holy Ghost came on them and they spake with tongues, and prophesied" (Acts 19:1-6).

Dear reader this same baptism of the Holy Spirit is available for you right now. Let's pray together. Jesus, thank you that you are my Lord and my Savior. Lord I want everything that you have to give me. I desire deep within me this same precious gift of the Holy Spirit that you poured out on your servants in that upper room. By faith and according to your word, baptize me and fill me right now with this same power from on high. Thank you, Lord!

KEY THREE:
LAYING ON OF HANDS

"And when Paul had laid his hands upon them, the Holy Ghost came on them and they spake with tongues, and prophesied" (Acts 19:6).

Paul teaches his new team the doctrine of the laying on of hands (Hebrews 6:2) and the power of apostolic impartation. There was a release of the Holy Spirit on these believers and they began to prophecy and speak in other tongues. Apostolic mantels release the gifts of the Spirit.

Paul said in Romans, "I desire to come unto you that I might impart some spiritual gift to the end you may be established" (Romans 1:11).

14 INSTANCES OF
THE LAYING ON OF HANDS

OLD TESTAMENT

1. The Priest laid his hands on the scapegoat as a means of transferring iniquity (Leviticus 1:4; Leviticus 16:21, 22).

The Apostolic Company

2. Jacob placed his hands upon Joseph's children to impart blessings (Genesis 48:14-16).

3. Moses imparted a portion of his wisdom and authority to Joshua by the laying on of hands at God's command. "And Joshua the son of Nun was full of the spirit of wisdom; for Moses had laid his hands upon him: and the children of Israel hearkened unto him, and did as the LORD commanded Moses" (Deuteronomy 34:9 KJV).

NEW TESTAMENT

Jesus our example:
4. In healing Jesus touched the leper. "And Jesus put forth his hand, and touched him, saying, I will; be thou clean. And immediately his leprosy was cleansed" (Matthew 8:3 KJV).

5. Jairus seeks Jesus to lay hands on his daughter. "And besought him greatly, saying, My little daughter lieth at the point of death: I pray thee, come and lay thy hands on her, that she may be healed; and she shall live" (Mark 5:23 KJV).

6. Jesus laid hands on the deaf. "And they bring unto him one that was deaf, and had an impediment in his speech; and they beseech him to put his hand upon him" (Mark 7:32 KJV).

7. In blessing the children. "And they brought young children to him, that he should touch them: and his disciples rebuked those that brought them" (Mark 10:13 KJV).

OTHER

8. Many Signs & Wonders. "And by the hands of the apostles were many signs and wonders wrought among the people; (and they were all with one accord in Solomon's porch" (Acts 5:12 KJV).

9. Receiving the Holy Spirit. "Then laid they their hands on them, and they received the Holy Ghost. {18} And when Simon saw that through laying on of the apostles' hands the Holy Ghost was given, he offered them money, {19} Saying, Give me also this power, that on whomsoever I lay hands, he may

receive the Holy Ghost" (Acts 8:17-19 KJV).

10. Healing of sight. "And Ananias went his way, and entered into the house; and putting his hands on him said, Brother Saul, the Lord, even Jesus, that appeared unto thee in the way as thou camest, hath sent me, that thou mightest receive thy sight, and be filled with the Holy Ghost" (Acts 9:17 KJV).

11. Apostolic Commission. "And when they had fasted and prayed, and laid their hands on them, they sent them away" (Acts 13:3 KJV).

12. More Signs & Wonders. "Long time therefore abode they speaking boldly in the Lord, which gave testimony unto the word of his grace, and granted signs and wonders to be done by their hands" (Acts 14:3 KJV).

13. Tongues & Prophesy. "And when Paul had laid his hands upon them, the Holy Ghost came on them; and they spake with tongues, and prophesied" (Acts 19:6 KJV).

14. Special Miracles. "And God wrought special miracles by the hands of Paul: {12} So that from his body were brought unto the sick handkerchiefs or aprons, and the diseases departed from them, and the evil spirits went out of them" (Acts 19:11-12 KJV).

APOSTOLIC BOLDNESS ALWAYS MANIFESTS ITSELF WHEN PERSECUTION ARISES BECAUSE OF THE GOSPEL.

KEY FOUR: BOLDNESS

"And all the men were about twelve. {8} And he went into the synagogue, and spake boldly for the space of three months, disputing and persuading the things concerning the kingdom of God. {9} But when divers were hardened, and believed not, but spake evil of that way before the multitude, he departed from them, and separated the disciples, disputing daily in the school of one

Tyrannus" (Acts 19:7-9 KJV). *Spiritual boldness is an apostolic trait.*

Here the newly founded team gets a chance to hear Paul speaking boldly in the synagogue during times of great conflict. Apostolic boldness always manifests itself when persecution arises because of the gospel.

The Holy Ghost loves boldness. To be bold shows a readiness to take risks, face danger, be daring and fearless. This is not a boldness worked up by man's soul but in fact is an evidence of being filled with the Holy Spirit and the manifestation of his grace. Another valuable lesson learned for this newly formed team.

4 EXAMPLES OF BOLDNESS

1. "The wicked flee when no man pursueth: but the righteous are bold as a lion" (Proverbs 28:1 KJV).

2. "And many of the brethren in the Lord, waxing confident by my bonds, are much more bold to speak the word without fear" (Philippians 1:14 KJV).

3. "But even after that we had suffered before, and were shamefully entreated, as ye know, at Philippi, we were bold in our

God to speak unto you the gospel of God with much contention" (1 Thessalonians 2:2 KJV).

4. "And now, Lord, behold their threatenings: and grant unto thy servants, that with all boldness they may speak thy word" (Acts 4:29 KJV).

AN APOSTOLIC GOVERNING CHURCH NEVER SUBSTITUTES DELIVERANCE WITH COUNSELING.

KEY FIVE: NO PREJUDICES

"And this continued by the space of two years; so that all they which dwelt in Asia heard the word of the Lord Jesus, both Jews and Greeks" (Acts 19:10 KJV). Paul, taking on the pattern from the Antioch believers, teaches that the gospel is not to the Jews only but also to the Greeks. He teaches them to breakthrough the walls of cultural separations, prejudice, preconceived ideas, and traditional patterns of ministry. It's unfortunate that people who say that they love God refuse to worship in multi-cultural settings.

KEY SIX: DELIVERANCE

"And God wrought special miracles by the hands of Paul: {12} So that from his body were brought unto the sick handkerchiefs or aprons, and the diseases departed from them, and the evil spirits went out of them" (Acts 19:11-12 KJV).

Paul is given the opportunity to demonstrate the miracle working power of God and teach the newly formed team about deliverance. You cannot have an apostolic governing church and ignore the devil. Sometimes abuse occurs in deliverance ministry, however, that doesn't mean we ignore its merits. Some people try to replace holy living and obedience with excuses for sinful behavior that can often be linked to generational curses, soul ties, witchcraft, etc. Therefore, our apostolic teams must be trained in spiritual warfare and deliverance. Jesus said that deliverance is the children's bread (Matthew 15:22,26) and Paul was very clear when he said, "Finally, my brethren, be strong in the Lord, and in the power of his might. {11} Put on the whole armor of God, that ye may be able to stand against the wiles of the devil. {12} For we wrestle not against flesh and blood, but against principalities, against powers, against the rulers of the darkness of this world, against spiritual wickedness in high places" (Ephesians 6:10-12 KJV).

Before Jesus sent out his apostolic teams, "he gave them power against unclean spirits, to cast them out, and to heal all manner of sickness and all manner of disease" (Matthew 10:1). *Jesus never taught his apostles to ignore the devil.* Jesus didn't leave them alone and neither should we. Demonic powers are still saying, "Let us alone; what have we to do with thee, thou Jesus of Nazareth? art thou come to destroy us? I know thee who thou art; the Holy One of God." Jesus' answer, "... hold thy peace, and come out of him. And when the devil had thrown him in the midst, he came out of him, and hurt him not" (Luke 4:34-35 KJV).

The cause of disease is often directly related to demonic activity as seen in the following scriptures.

> "How God anointed Jesus of Nazareth with the Holy Ghost and with power: who went about doing good, and healing all that were oppressed of the devil; for God was with him" (Acts 10:38 KJV).

> "There came also a multitude out of the cities round about unto

The Apostolic Company

Jerusalem, bringing sick folks, and them which were vexed with unclean spirits: and they were healed every one" (Acts 5:16 KJV).

Understanding our authority as believers in spiritual warfare and deliverance is very important to the apostolic team. Spiritual warfare is simply binding and loosing in prayer and attacking on purpose spiritual strongholds of opposition and resistance to the advancement of the gospel in a territory (Matthew 18:18-20). It is a taking up, in prayer, the authority of the believer that Jesus gave to his church (Luke 10:17-20). It is having faith in God. This is all with the understanding that we are not wrestling with people, but with principalities, powers, rulers of darkness of this world and spiritual wickedness in high places (Ephesians 6:12).

Deliverance and the casting out of demons is the first sign that should follow the believer. As it is written, "and these signs shall follow them that believe; In my name shall they cast out devils ..." (Mark 16:17 KJV). An apostolic governing church never substitutes deliverance with counseling.

This is not to say that they won't counsel, they will. However, an apostolic church will flow in the anointing that sets the captives free.

OPERATING IN DELIVERANCE, SPIRITUAL AUTHORITY, AND SPIRITUAL WARFARE WITH BALANCE IS AN INTRICATE AND VITAL PART OF AN APOSTOLIC CHURCH.

There are many different types of prayer in the word of God, all of which are given to us for Spirit life living and for the advancement of the gospel (Ephesians 6:18). All are apostolic weapons and tools available for the advancement of the gospel.

12 DIFFERENT TYPES OF PRAYER

1. Prayer That Doesn't Give Up -- Importunity (Luke 18:6-8).
2. Prayer Of Faith (James 5:15; Matthew 21:22; Mark 11:24).
3. Deliverance Prayer (Acts 16:18).

4. Binding & Loosing (Matthew 16:19).
5. Prayer of Agreement (Matthew 18:18-20; Leviticus 26:8).
6. Praying in the Spirit, Tongues (Jude 20; 1 Corinthians 14:4, 14:14-15; Isaiah 28:11-12; Acts 10:46).
7. Fervent Effective Prayer (James 5:16; Romans 12:11; Colossians 4:12).
8. Prayer of Consecration & Dedication (Luke 22:42).
9. Prayer of Commitment (1 Peter 5:7).
10. Prayer of Worship (Luke 24:52-53; Acts 13:1-4).
11. Corporate Prayer (Acts 4:23-31).
12. Prayer with Groanings & Travail (Romans 8:26; Isaiah 66:8; Galations 4:19; Jeremiah 30:6).

WARFARE IS THE BRIDGE

Spiritual warfare uses all the various types of prayer at our disposal. Often I hear people bashing those that teach the truths about deliverance or spiritual warfare. The problem with that is two-fold.

First, you cannot receive that which you mock and attack.

Second, spiritual warfare and deliverance is the very bridge needed to cross over in order to become fully apostolic.

During the 1980's, the church began moving into a deeper understanding of the need for spiritual warfare and deliverance. The 1990's brought a restoration of the ministry of the prophet. The 21st Century is experiencing the restoration of the apostle with a deeper understanding of the prophetic. Spiritual warfare and deliverance were the bridge from the teaching ministry that was so prominent in the 70's, to the apostolic restoration of today. Operating in deliverance, spiritual authority, and spiritual warfare with balance is an intricate and vital part of an apostolic church.

SPIRIT-FILLED CHRISTIANS CANNOT CONTINUE TO AVOID SPIRITUAL CONFLICT, WHILE HIDING BEHIND A COMFORTABLE AND OFTENTIMES BACKSLIDDEN CONDITION.

The Apostolic Company

Apostles must be prepared to meet strong opposition from Satan and the occult influences in society (1 Thessalonians 2:18). The prophet Daniel was told, "Fear not, Daniel: for from the first day that thou didst set thine heart to understand, and to chasten thyself before thy God, thy words were heard, and I am come for thy words. {13} But the prince of the kingdom of Persia withstood me one and twenty days: but, lo, Michael, one of the chief princes, came to help me; and I remained there with the kings of Persia. {14} Now I am come to make thee understand what shall befall thy people in the latter days: for yet the vision is for many days" (Daniel 10:12-14 KJV).

Spirit-filled Christians cannot continue to avoid spiritual conflict, while hiding behind a comfortable and oftentimes backslidden condition. To do this ignores the needs of those around us. Opposition, persecution and resistance are all part of the package. Paul declared, "For a great door and effectual is opened unto me, and there are many adversaries" (1 Corinthians 16:9 KJV). The effective advancement of the gospel always causes a reaction. Why do we need a firm understanding in this area? Let's look at some of the negative reactions to apostolic ministry.

REACTIONS
TO APOSTOLIC MINISTRY

1. In Antioch-Pisidia -- *Persecution*
"And the next sabbath day came almost the whole city together to hear the word of God. {45} But when the Jews saw the multitudes, they were filled with envy, and spake against those things which were spoken by Paul, contradicting and blaspheming .... But the Jews stirred up the devout and honorable women, and the chief men of the city, and raised persecution against Paul and Barnabas, and expelled them out of their coasts" (Acts 13:44-45,50 KJV).

2. In Iconium -- *Assault*
"And it came to pass in Iconium, that they went both together into the synagogue of the Jews, and so spake, that a great multitude both of the Jews and also of the Greeks believed. {2} But the unbelieving Jews stirred up the Gentiles, and made their minds evil affected against the brethren. {3} Long time therefore abode they speaking

boldly in the Lord, which gave testimony unto the word of his grace, and granted signs and wonders to be done by their hands. {4} But the multitude of the city was divided: and part held with the Jews, and part with the apostles. {5} And when there was an assault made both of the Gentiles, and also of the Jews with their rulers, to use them despitefully, and to stone them, {6} They were aware of it, and fled unto Lystra and Derbe, cities of Lycaonia, and unto the region that lieth round about" (Acts 14:1-6 KJV).

3. Lystra -- *Stoning*
"And there came thither certain Jews from Antioch and Iconium, who persuaded the people, and, having stoned Paul, drew him out of the city, supposing he had been dead. {20} Howbeit, as the disciples stood round about him, he rose up, and came into the city: and the next day he departed with Barnabas to Derbe" (Acts 14:19-20 KJV).

4. *Persecution & Affliction*
"But thou hast fully known my doctrine, manner of life, purpose,

Governing Churches

faith, longsuffering, charity, patience, {11} Persecutions, afflictions, which came unto me at Antioch, at Iconium, at Lystra; what persecutions I endured: but out of them all the Lord delivered me. {12} Yea, and all that will live godly in Christ Jesus shall suffer persecution. {13} But evil men and seducers shall wax worse and worse, deceiving, and being deceived. {14} But continue thou in the things which thou hast learned and hast been assured of, knowing of whom thou hast learned them" (2 Timothy 3:10-14 KJV).

5.) In Philippi -- *Shamefully Treated*
"But even after that we had suffered before, and were shamefully entreated, as ye know, at Philippi, we were bold in our God to speak unto you the gospel of God with much contention" (1 Th 2:2 KJV).

6.) In Thessalonica -- *Fines*
"And when they found them not, they drew Jason and certain brethren unto the rulers of the city, crying, These that have turned the world upside down are come hither also ... And when they had taken

security of Jason, and of the other, they let them go" (Acts 17:6,9 KJV).

(Jason was probably required to put up property or post a bond as a guarantee toward keeping peace in the city.)

7. In Berea -- *Opposition*
"But when the Jews of Thessalonica had knowledge that the word of God was preached of Paul at Berea, they came thither also, and stirred up the people" (Acts 17:13 KJV).

A fully functioning apostolic ministry causes a stir in the city as it moves forward with a compelling and invading gospel that fulfills Jesus' commandment, "occupy till I come" (Luke 19:13).

KEY SEVEN: DIAKONEO

"After these things were ended, Paul purposed in the spirit, when he had passed through Macedonia and Achaia, to go to Jerusalem, saying, After I have been there, I must also see Rome. {22} So he sent into Macedonia two of them that ministered unto him, Timotheus and

Erastus; but he himself stayed in Asia for a season" (Acts 19:21-22 KJV).

Here Paul completes the apostolic pattern of...

gathering

teaching

training

sending forth

Paul chooses Timotheus and Erastus who had ministered unto him. Until you have learned how to serve someone else, you can never be sent forth.

Minister, from the Greek *minus* or *minor*, means one who acts as an inferior agent in obedience or subservience to another, or who serves or officiates in contrast to the master (from *magnus*) or superior. This Greek word for ministered (*diakoneo*) is closely related to the English word deacon meaning to serve.

Erastus could be the same person discussed in Romans 16:23 and referred to as the chamberlain of the city, or the city manager. He must have been a remarkable man.

The Holy Spirit is opening our eyes to the use of apostolic teams in the word of God. We used to think about Paul only, or

The Apostolic Company

Peter only, but now we see that the Holy Spirit formed teams like...

Paul and Barnabas (Acts 13:43, 46)

Paul and Silas (Acts 16:19)

Paul, Barnabas, Judas, and Silas (Acts 15:22)

Peter and John (Acts 3:1)

Paul and Timotheus (Philippians 1:1)

Paul and Silvanus and Timotheus (Acts 16:19)

Paul and Company - Team (Acts 13:13)

Even though God pulled together teams, he did not use just anybody. Next, we will look at the qualifications of those apostolic team members.

Governing Churches

☐ If we are going to see the manifestation of the glorious church, (Ephesians 5:27) then we obviously need to have a structural change in the way we reach our cities.

☐ One of the main requirements of a team member is they must be teachable.

☐ Apostles have the anointing to pull together disciples and put them to work as a team.

☐ Apostolic mantels release the gifts of the Spirit.

☐ To be bold shows a readiness to take risks, face danger, be daring and fearless.

☐ Jesus never taught his apostles to ignore the devil.

☐ An apostolic governing church will never substitute deliverance with counseling.

☐ Operating in deliverance, spiritual authority, and spiritual

The Apostolic Company

warfare is an intricate and vital part of an apostolic church.

☐ Minister, from the Greek *minus* or *minor,* means one who acts as an inferior agent in obedience or subservience to another, or who serves or officiates in contrast to the master, Greek *magnus,* or superior.

Governing Churches

CHAPTER 11
EARMARKS OF APOSTOLIC TEAMS

Apostles have the ability to press through during times of intense spiritual battles because they have learned that battles first must be fought in the spirit realm before they can be won in the natural realm.

L et's discuss more fully the qualifications of apostolic teams found in the book of Thessalonians. Our culture values individual accomplishment, and encourages and promotes individualism. We typically compete against one another for job advancements, in sports, and all sorts of other activities.

Competing with one another is not allowed within apostolic churches because there is no promotion of individual stardom. Although it is appropriate to acknowledge that there are team leaders, the mission of the team does not depend on one team member alone. Apostolic people are masters at cooperation with one another. This principle is even evident in the team work of the trinity as well.

Paul described how he and his apostolic team entered the city of Thessalonica. We often fail to realize that Paul had a team with him. The opening text of First Thessalonians reads, "Paul, *and* Silvanus, *and* Timotheus, unto the church of the Thessalonians ..." (1 Thessalonians 1:1). Notice the use of the word and.

APOSTOLIC PEOPLE HAVE LEARNED THAT BATTLES MUST FIRST BE FOUGHT IN THE SPIRIT REALM BEFORE THEY CAN BE WON IN THE NATURAL REALM.

TIMES OF CONTENTION

Scripture reveals that the team members were familiar with suffering and had been treated badly in Philippi.

"For yourselves, brethren, know our entrance in unto you, that it was not in vain: {2} But even after that we had suffered before, and were shamefully entreated, as ye know, at Philippi, we were bold in our God to speak unto you the gospel of God with much contention" (1 Thessalonians 2:1-2 KJV).

However, the team didn't give up and quit but continued on with boldness to speak the gospel, even during times of great contention. The contention spoken of here goes well beyond people who might have caused them trouble, and reaches into the realm of spiritual warfare. This word contention, Greek *agon* reveals the condition of the spiritual climate of the territory -- hard (Deuteronomy 28:23).

GOD'S CHOICE FOR A TEAM MEMBER IS IDENTIFIED FIRST BY CHARACTER AND SECOND BY ANOINTINGS.

Throughout my travels preaching the gospel in various countries, I have noticed that there are three primary spiritual climates. They are ...

hard

harder

hardest

Unfortunately, there are no longer any easy places of ministry.

The word *agon* is taken from the root word *ago* meaning to take the lead. Paul and team took the lead in attacking the spiritual climate of the territory, which was filled with ...

great conflict

fight

contention

struggle

spiritual battle

However, Paul and the team pressed through because of the anointing on them that brings victory. The word contention *(agon)* also denotes a contest for victory (i.e., the Grecian games of running, wrestling, and boxing) or a battle that could be life threatening and involves great danger.

This same spiritual conflict *(agon)* we face today. It is real, and is much more than an irritation because the pastor didn't smile at you or someone was rude to your child at the Christian academy last week. This is real spiritual conflict.

Apostolic ministry has the noteworthy trait of being able to press through during times of intense spiritual battles that manifest on the earth through people. What is in the territory, spiritually, will walk into your church and say, "Hi." Apostolic people have learned that battles must first be fought in the spirit realm before they can be won in the natural realm.

Apostolic teams don't wait for the battle to come to them, they are go first pioneers, that will take the sword of the Spirit to the battle.

We have already discussed boldness and spiritual warfare, so let's review some of the other qualifications of apostolic team members.

11 QUALIFICATIONS FOR APOSTOLIC TEAM MEMBERS

When studying the requirements for apostolic teams, character must be examined closely. Training, maturity, and experience are all important, but more importantly is the foundation of a person, his character. *God's choice for a team member is identified first by character and second by anointings.*

Governing Churches

The apostle Peter puts things in perspective when he says, "add to your faith virtue" (2 Peter 1:5).

Scripture shows us the qualifications for apostolic teams. "For our exhortation was not of deceit, nor of uncleanness, nor in guile" (1 Thessalonians 2:3 KJV).

1. Honest and Transparent
"... was not of deceit."

To deceive means to seduce one into believing that something is true when it is not or to just simply lie. People who are liars cannot serve on apostolic teams. Paul says, "Therefore seeing we have this ministry, as we have received mercy, we faint not; {2} But have renounced the hidden things of dishonesty, not walking in craftiness, nor handling the word of God deceitfully; but by manifestation of the truth commending ourselves to every man's conscience in the sight of God" (2 Corinthians 4:1-2 KJV). False apostles and prophets minister out of a deceitful heart. "Then the LORD said unto me, The prophets prophesy lies in my name: I sent them not, neither have I commanded them, neither spake unto them: they prophesy unto you a false vision and divination, and a thing of nought, and the deceit of their heart" (Jeremiah 14:14 KJV).

2. Pure Motives
"... nor of uncleanness."

The team member must not have an air of uncleanness about them. This scripture implies that they have impure motives. *The member should never use the apostolic team as a means to promote their own ministry.* This is totally unacceptable and a violation of the team spirit. "For God hath not called us unto uncleanness, but unto holiness" (1 Thessalonians 4:7 KJV).

3. Upright
"... nor in guile."

To minister in guile means to be...

crafty

slick

cunning

Governing Churches

tricky

playing all the games

testing the boundaries

Team members must be people of character, honesty, and trust. Notice that all of these things deal with a team member's character rather than religious education or even anointings.

"But as we were allowed of God to be put in trust with the gospel, even so we speak; not as pleasing men, but God, which trieth our hearts" (1 Thessalonians 2:4 KJV).

4. A God Pleaser
"... not as pleasing men."

Many people fall into the trap of trying to please men. This is an indication that they are not free from the snares of pride. Therefore, they never say anything provoking or deemed controversial because they are fearful of how men would view them. The fear of man disqualifies one from being on an apostolic team.

King Saul feared the people more than he reverenced God and

Earmarks Of Apostolic Teams

because he was full of rebellion, he lost the kingdom. "And Saul said unto Samuel, I have sinned: for I have transgressed the commandment of the LORD, and thy words: because I feared the people, and obeyed their voice. And Samuel said unto him, The LORD hath rent the kingdom of Israel from thee this day, and hath given it to a neighbor of thine, that is better than thou" (1 Samuel 15:24,28 KJV).

The fear of man will cause you to compromise your faith in an attempt to keep a position or it can create an intimidation that will quiet your testimony. Peter and the other apostles displayed an apostolic fortitude when challenged with the fear of men, "And when they had brought them, they set them before the council: and the high priest asked them, {28} Saying, Did not we straitly command you that ye should not teach in this name? and, behold, ye have filled Jerusalem with your doctrine, and intend to bring this man's blood upon us. {29} Then Peter and the other apostles answered and said, We ought to obey God rather than men" (Acts 5:27-29 KJV). The high calling on an apostolic team is to obey God.

5. Without Flattering Words

"*For neither at any time used we flattering words*, as ye know, nor a cloak of covetousness; God is witness" (1 Thessalonians 2:5 KJV Italics added).

This Scripture does not say that someone cannot be given a compliment for a job well done. Everyone enjoys a compliment and some encouragement. However, it does address the use of flattering words used as a cloak of covetousness to deceive, control, or to manipulate. We should never use flattery as a means to deceive or control, nor can we afford to be moved by flattery. This is very dangerous and very inappropriate, and potentially quite harmful. The word tells us, "know we no man after the flesh..." (2 Corinthians 5:16 KJV).

Three Examples Of Vain Flattery

"They speak vanity every one with his neighbor: with flattering lips and with a double heart do they speak. {3} The LORD shall cut off all flattering lips, and the tongue that speaketh proud things" (Psalms 12:2-3 KJV).

"A man that flattereth his neighbor spreadeth a net for his feet" (Proverbs 29:5 KJV).

"For when they speak great swelling words of vanity, they allure through the lusts of the flesh, through much wantonness, those that were clean escaped from them who live in error" (2 Peter 2:18 KJV).

6. Not Greedy
"... nor a cloak of covetousness."

A cloak of covetousness refers to using flattering words for the sake of gaining what belongs to others because of greed. God does not want us to be selfish or self-centered. We must be people willing to meet the needs of others. To be greedy means to take all that you can without the thought or consideration of others. This scripture associates flattering words with someone who would use the deception of flattery for gaining money. The motive of apostolic teams is never financial gain!

The word even goes as far as warning us of the possible deception of titles. "Let me not, I pray you, accept any man's person, neither let me give flattering titles unto man. {22} For I know not to give flattering titles; in so doing my maker would soon take me away" (Job 32:21-22 KJV).

"Nor of men sought we glory, neither of you, nor yet of others, when we might have been burdensome, as the apostles of Christ" (1 Thessalonians 2:6 KJV).

7. Avoiding honor, praise, recognition of men, titles, etc.
"... nor of men sought we glory."

The scriptures are clear that we should never think more highly of ourselves that we ought (1 Peter 5:3). Jesus said, "I receive not honour from men" (John 5:41 KJV). Apostolic teams are not working for merit badges, awards, plagues, or praise of men; they are obeying the leading of the Holy

Earmarks Of Apostolic Teams

Spirit. Recognition by men is not the issue, the purpose for being on the team is...

to reach the lost

advance the gospel

and complete the apostolic vision for the territory.

Jesus focuses us by declaring, "How can ye believe, which receive honour one of another, and seek not the honour that cometh from God only?" (John 5:44 KJV). The scriptures also warn us of the behavior of the Pharisees, "Nevertheless among the chief rulers also many believed on him; but because of the Pharisees they did not confess him, lest they should be put out of the synagogue: {43} For they loved the praise of men more than the praise of God" (John 12:42-43 KJV).

"For do I now persuade men, or God? or do I seek to please men? for if I yet pleased men, I should not be the servant of Christ" (Galations 1:10 KJV).

"Put not forth thyself in the presence of the king, and stand not in the place of great men: {7} For better it is that it be said unto thee, Come up hither; than that thou shouldest be put lower in the presence of the prince whom thine eyes have seen" (Proverbs 25:6-7 KJV).

"But we were gentle among you, even as a nurse cherisheth her children: {8} So being affectionately desirous of you, we were willing to have imparted unto you, not the gospel of God only, but also our own souls, because ye were dear unto us" (1 Thessalonians 2:7-8 KJV).

8. Gentle
"But we were gentle ..."

The team member should be gentle, with a servant's heart, not pushy. To be gentle (not to be confused with weak) means to be affectionately desirous with a longing of love for your brothers and sisters in Christ. Team members are not to be lords over God's heritage, but be examples to the flock (1 Peter 5:3 KJV). Jesus said, "Take my yoke upon you, and learn of me; for I am meek and lowly in heart: and ye shall find rest unto your souls. {30} For my yoke is easy, and my burden is light" (Matthew 11:29-30 KJV). "And the servant of the Lord must not strive; but be gentle unto all men, apt to teach, patient, {25} In meekness instructing those that oppose themselves; if God peradventure will give them repentance to the acknowledging of the truth" (2 Timothy 2:24-25 KJV).

Jesus shows us the heart of a shepherd when he declares, "He shall feed his flock like a shepherd: he shall gather the lambs with his arm, and carry them in his bosom, and shall gently lead those that are with young" (Isaiah 40:11 KJV).

"For ye remember, brethren, our labour and travail: for laboring night and day, because we would not be chargeable unto any of you, we preached unto you the gospel of God" (1 Thessalonians 2:9 KJV).

9. Hard Workers
"... laboring night and day ..."

Governing Churches

Laziness has no place on an apostolic team. People who want to be on an apostolic team simply to get away for a season or just go on holiday must not be allowed on the team. Apostolic ministry teams consist of hard workers, not sluggards using the ministry to support their slothfulness. Team members must be able to work hard, endure hardship as good soldiers (2 Timothy 2:3), and have a willingness to serve. I have seen many who have traveled to the nations only to complain about inadequate hotel accommodations, water, air conditioning, food, etc. "Yea, ye yourselves know, that these hands have ministered unto my necessities, and to them that were with me. {35} I have showed you all things, how that so labouring ye ought to support the weak, and to remember the words of the Lord Jesus, how he said, It is more blessed to give than to receive" (Acts 20:34-35 KJV).

"Ye are witnesses, and God also, how holily and justly and unblameably we behaved ourselves among you that believe" (1 Thessalonians 2:10 KJV).

Earmarks Of Apostolic Teams

10. Holy & Just
"... holy and justly ..."

We don't hear the word holiness used much anymore, but it is certainly a main qualification for placement on an apostolic team. Holy living is of the utmost importance in serving God and advancing the gospel. In the context of this verse it means to be undefiled by sin, free from lust, wickedness, etc. while diligently observing every moral obligation. This verse also gives reference to outward appearance and the manner of one's dress. We often see people dress in the ungodly fashion of the day, which is totally inappropriate and a reflection of worldly living and carnal mindedness. Paul boldly advises us, "But I keep under my body, and bring it into subjection: lest that by any means, when I have preached to others, I myself should be a castaway" (1 Corinthians 9:27 KJV). We are not called to fashion ourselves like the world (Romans 12:1-2).

11. Blameless
"... unblameably we behaved ..."

Governing Churches

To be blameless means to be free from the appearance of evil or other inappropriate behavior that would disqualify a person from the team. It also means that the team member is not a fault finder or one who critiques others.

"And they were both righteous before God, walking in all the commandments and ordinances of the Lord blameless" (Luke 1:6 KJV).

"To the end he may stablish your hearts unblameable in holiness before God, even our Father, at the coming of our Lord Jesus Christ with all his saints" (1 Thessalonians 3:13 KJV).

"And the very God of peace sanctify you wholly; and I pray God your whole spirit and soul and body be preserved blameless unto the coming of our Lord Jesus Christ" (1 Thessalonians 5:23 KJV).

Finally, an apostolic team should set a fine example for others. Paul said, "For yourselves know how ye ought to follow us: for we behaved not ourselves disorderly among you; {8} Neither did we eat any man's bread for nought; but wrought with labour and travail night and day, that we might not be chargeable to any of you: {9} Not because we have not power, but to make ourselves an ensample unto you to follow us" (2 Thessalonians 3:7-9 KJV).

Now that we have examined the earmarks of apostolic teams, let's take a look at 14 earmarks of an apostolic church.

14 EARMARKS OF AN APOSTOLIC CHURCH

1. Multi-cultural churches
Apostolic churches consist of a multiplicity of cultures, skin colors, and social status. Everyone is important and no one is better than another.

2. Without racism or prejudices
They have the ability to break out of their own prejudices and any traditions or prejudices in their territory.

3. Inter-related churches
Everybody is important. *The Antioch governing churches are champions of cooperation.* They value various giftings and are not threatened or intimated by others. They understand the power of

working together in a type of synergy (1 Corinthians 12:20, Ephesians 4:16).

4. Apostolic structure of leadership

Typically, apostolic churches have one set man (Numbers 27:16) and elders consisting of prophets and teachers that make up a presbytery. They are not bless me only models of churches, but are build me, mature me, and send me models. The New Testament clearly establishes that all believers constitute a ministering priesthood (1 Peter 2:9). The apostolic structure is filled with team ministries.

5. Evangelistic churches

Apostolic churches break out of the four walls of the sanctuary onto the streets and into the homes to preach the gospel. It is not about bringing the lost to the church for the pastor to lead them in the sinner's prayer, but to take the gospel to them.

6. Visible grace on them

The grace and favor of God are upon the apostolic churches as a visible working of the gifts of the Spirit. It is impossible to have a visible grace upon a ministry unless that ministry is walking in liberty (Galations 5:1).

"Now concerning spiritual gifts, brethren, I would not have you ignorant. {2} Ye know that ye were Gentiles, carried away unto these dumb idols, even as ye were led. {3} Wherefore I give you to understand, that no man speaking by the Spirit of God calleth Jesus accursed: and that no man can say that Jesus is the Lord, but by the Holy Ghost. {4} Now there are diversities of gifts, but the same Spirit. {5} And there are differences of administrations, but the same Lord. {6} And there are diversities of operations, but it is the same God which worketh all in all. {7} But the manifestation of the Spirit is given to every man to profit withal. {8} For to one is given by the Spirit the word of wisdom; to another the word of knowledge by the same Spirit; {9} To another faith by the same Spirit; to another the gifts of healing by the same Spirit; {10} To another the working of miracles; to another prophecy; to another discerning of spirits; to another divers kinds of tongues; to another the interpretation of tongues: {11} But all these worketh that one and the selfsame Spirit, dividing to every man severally as he will" (1 Corinthians 12:1-11 KJV).

7. Honor and receive others

The Antioch believers received Barnabas and Paul. Unfortunately, in some countries ministers are received according to how much money they can bring with them, but apostolic churches recognize the anointing and calling upon the lives of others. It is not what they can do for them naturally, but what they carry spiritually.

> "Then Peter said, Silver and gold have I none; but such as I have give I thee: In the name of Jesus Christ of Nazareth rise up and walk" (Acts 3:6 KJV).

8. Prophetic teaching and training centers

Apostolic churches are teaching and training centers. Clearly, prophets and teachers first led the Antioch church. Barnabas and Paul taught there for a year before being sent (Acts 11:26). We shall see many teaching resource materials birthed in apostolic churches.

9. Giving churches

Apostolic churches are giving churches who respond to financial needs and the advancement of the ministry like no other. The church in Antioch responded with a great gift to their brothers in need in Judaea.

> "Then the disciples, every man according to his ability, determined to send relief unto the brethren which dwelt in Judaea: {30} Which also they did, and sent it to the elders by the hands of Barnabas and Saul" (Acts 11:29-30 KJV).

10. Sending churches

The Antioch church was the first church to *prophetically* send out a team of apostles.

11. Praying Churches

One of the greatest signs of an apostolic church is their corporate and private prayer life.

> "And he taught, saying unto them, Is it not written, My house shall be called of all nations the house of prayer?" (Mark 11:17 KJV).

12. Fasting Churches

Apostolic churches are fasting churches. Because of the heavy opposition against them they often are led by the Holy Spirit into times of fasting and prayer.

"Is not this the fast that I have chosen? to loose the bands of wickedness, to undo the heavy burdens, and to let the oppressed go free, and that ye break every yoke?" (Isa 58:6 KJV).

13. Supernatural Churches

Apostolic churches are supernatural churches. Paul declares, "And my speech and my preaching was not with enticing words of man's wisdom, but in demonstration of the Spirit and of power: {5} That your faith should not stand in the wisdom of men, but in the power of God" (1 Corinthians 2:4-5 KJV).

The word tells us that, "by the hands of the apostles were many signs and wonders wrought among the people; (and they were all with one accord in Solomon's porch" (Acts 5:12 KJV). Then when pressed with persecution, "By stretching forth thine hand to heal; and that signs and wonders may be done by the name of thy holy child Jesus" (Acts 4:30 KJV).

14. Spirit Life Builders

Whereas the religious look to soulish activity, programs, and man's philosophy, the apostolic look to the Holy Spirit for guidance. David told his son Solomon that the pattern for the temple came from the Spirit of God (1 Chronicles 12:28). So it is

Earmarks Of Apostolic Teams

today with apostolic ministry and churches, they are Spirit led (Romans 8).

For a more detailed list of the qualities of an apostolic church read my book, *50 Earmarks of an Apostolic Church*. In this book you will discover how to identify an apostolic ministry in your city.

In the next chapter we will discover that apostolic gifts come alive in the midst of adversity.

Governing Churches

SUMMARY: EARMARKS OF APOSTOLIC TEAMS

☐ Scripture says that a requirement for apostolic teams is discipleship.

☐ A noteworthy trait of apostolic ministry is their ability to press through during times of intense spiritual battles.

☐ Apostolic churches consist of a multiplicity of cultures, skin colors, and social status. Everyone is important and no one is better than another.

☐ Antioch governing churches are champions of cooperation.

☐ Apostolic churches are teaching and training centers.

☐ The Antioch church was the first church to *prophetically* send out a team of apostles.

☐ Apostolic churches are supernatural churches.

CHAPTER 12
UZZIAH THE
REFORMER

Apostolic gifts have a strong inner strength that continues to speak, "God is able." No matter how hard the situation gets, their gifts seem to come alive in the midst of adversity proclaiming that God is able.

King Uzziah demonstrated an apostolic pattern in his life and work by being a builder as well as a restorer. Apostolic ministry gifts are builders and will carry a divine ability to restore.

"Then all the people of Judah took Uzziah, who was sixteen years old, and made him king in the room of his father Amaziah. {2} He built Eloth, and restored it to Judah, after that the king slept with his fathers" (2 Chronicles 26:1-2 KJV).

To restore (*shuwb*) means to turn back, recover, or to return again. There are certain truths that have been lost in the sea of the religious traditions of men that God is restoring through the apostolic church. We can learn some important truths by examining the life of King Uzziah as he brought forth a reforming spirit into Judah.

GOD IS ALWAYS ABLE

"Sixteen years old was Uzziah when he began to reign, and he reigned fifty and two years in Jerusalem. His mother's name also was Jecoliah of Jerusalem" (2 Chronicles 26:3 KJV).

THE SECRET TO THE SUCCESS OF APOSTOLIC MINISTRY IS SEEKING GOD.

Uzziah's mother was Jecoliah, which translated means God is able. Imagine all your young life hearing your mother's name being called. "God is able. God is able!" Even from a young age the Spirit of God was putting a great foundational truth into Uzziah's life that, "God is able to make all grace abound toward you; that you, always having all sufficiency in all things, may abound to every good work" (2 Corinthians 9:8 KJV).

Apostolic gifts have a strong inner strength that continues to speak, "God is able." No matter how hard the situation gets, their gifts seem to come alive in the midst of adversity proclaiming Jecoliah, that God is able. "Now unto him that is able to do exceeding abundantly above all that we ask or think, according to the power that worketh in us" (Ephesians 3:20 KJV).

STAYING RIGHT IN THE SIGHT OF THE LORD

"And he did that which was right in the sight of the LORD, according to all that his father Amaziah did" (2 Chronicles 26:4 KJV). Uzziah did that which was right in the sight of the Lord. This means that he lived a righteous life and did that which was pleasing to God. It also means that he was straight with his business dealings and with other people.

CHANGE, NOT BLESSING ONLY, IS THE WORD OF THE LORD FOR THE 21ST CENTURY CHURCH.

The apostolic anointing is released toward those who allow the Spirit of God to work on developing a righteous character in them. Character has nothing to do with reputation, which is what others think about you, but rather character is what God knows about you.

Many people seek the anointing and blessing of God, but solid Christian character enables one to carry it. Change, not blessing only, is the word of the Lord for the 21st Century church.

SEEKING GOD IS THE SECRET

"And he sought God in the days of Zechariah, who had understanding in the visions of God: and as long as he sought the LORD, God made him to prosper" (2 Chronicles 26:5 KJV). The secret to the success of apostolic ministry is seeking God.

To seek out (*darash*) means to...

consult

inquire of

ask

commune

seek

194

pursue

As long as Uzziah sought God, he prospered. This word prosper (*tsalach*) refers not only to wealth, but also means to advance, make progress, succeed and to profit at all you put your hands to do. *The key to apostolic ministry's success is the ability to continually put the Lord first.* Seeking God releases divine authority and an anointing to succeed in ministry, purpose and whatever you put your hand to do.

WARS, WALLS, BUILDINGS

"And he went forth and warred against the Philistines, and brake down the wall of Gath, and the wall of Jabneh, and the wall of Ashdod, and built cities about Ashdod, and among the Philistines. {7} And God helped him against the Philistines, and against the Arabians that dwelt in Gurbaal, and the Mehunims" (2 Chronicles 26:6-7 KJV).

Three key abilities of apostolic ministry are found in this verse.

1. Uzziah went to war against the Philistines with the assistance of God. This is a powerful key; God helped Uzziah with

with supernatural assistance against the Philistines, who were old enemies of Israel. Throughout the world, there are principalities and powers who have stood against the advancement of the gospel and the church. They are old enemies, but the Spirit of God is raising up those who have the conquering anointing that King Uzziah carried to fight them. Old enemies are about to be conquered by the restoration of the apostolic governing church. So, don't let it enter your heart that just because they have been around for a long time they are there to stay. The apostolic anointing has a divine empowerment to conquer even old enemies.

APOSTOLIC MINISTRY GIFTS, RATHER THAN DISCOURAGE, WILL CALL ALONGSIDE, GIVE PLACE TO, LIFT UP AND STRENGTHEN THE PROPHETIC MINISTRY.

---

2. We also see that Uzziah broke down the wall of Gath. As mentioned before, one of the key gifts of apostolic ministry is their ability to break down the walls in the

spirit that divide. Walls are what keep the gospel in or out and divide or separate people from one another. There are many walls, including:

prejudice

religious traditions

language

social class or cast systems

racism

forms

traditions

ceremonies

Uzziah, with an apostolic anointing, broke down those walls that were symbolic of demonic reinforcement and strength.

3. Uzziah also built cities about Ashdod and among the Philistines, which is a prophetic type for us to see. *God gives apostolic ministry strategy and ability to build strongholds of ministry, even in the midst of our enemies.* It doesn't matter how hard the territory, God will do whatever it takes to build his church and the gates of

hell shall not prevail. With every territorial assignment comes sufficient grace to fulfill your calling.

"But unto every one of us is given grace according to the measure of the gift of Christ" (Ephesians 4:7).

TIME FOR TRIBUTE

"And the Ammonites gave gifts to Uzziah: and his name spread abroad even to the entering in of Egypt; for he strengthened himself exceedingly" (2 Chronicles 26:8 KJV). People often get weary of spiritual warfare, but I've got good news for you. When you win, you get the spoil! Here we see the Ammonites bringing gifts to Uzziah. This word gifts (*minchah*) is better translated as tribute.

Tribute is the regular payment of money made by one ruler or nation to another as acknowledgment of subjugation.

The apostolic call has the anointing to dominate and subdue (Genesis 1:28). To bring their enemies into subjugation. Are you ready to receive some tribute?

Subdue means to invade and bring into subjugation. When the Ammonites gave gifts to Uzziah, it was an acknowledgment

198

that he had subdued them. The wealth of the sinner is laid up for the just (Proverbs 13:22). Are you ready for it to transfer?

PROPHETIC TOWERS

"Moreover Uzziah built towers in Jerusalem at the corner gate, and at the valley gate, and at the turning of the wall, and fortified them. {10} Also he built towers in the desert, and digged many wells: for he had much cattle, both in the low country, and in the plains: husbandmen also, and vine dressers in the mountains, and in Carmel: for he loved husbandry" (2 Chronicles 26:9-10 KJV).

APOSTOLIC LEADERS KNOW HOW TO BUILD A SPIRIT OF PRAYER IN THE LIFE OF THE CHURCH.

Uzziah built towers, which is an apostolic pattern; a type of the prophetic ministry. *Apostles are the gifts that God is using to build the platforms for the prophetic voice.* Towers are for...

watching

warning

seeing

listening

signaling

Towers are also symbolic for the platform of prophetic ministry. The prophetic ministry is given the responsibility of...

watching

seeing

hearing

saying

Apostolic ministry gifts are not afraid of the prophets, and will build towers or platforms of ministry, providing the prophetic a place to operate fully in their gifting.

Uzziah fortified the towers he built. To fortify means to strengthen or to give strength to. Apostolic ministry gifts, rather than discourage, will call alongside, give place to, lift up and strengthen the prophetic ministry.

Uzziah The Reformer

Uzziah also dug many wells. Without water, there can be no life. Apostolic gifts have the ability to dig wells even in desert places where it is spiritually dry. God is anointing the apostolic gifts to go into spiritually dry places and dig wells of life so that God's people can be refreshed with His word. Spiritual wells are dug through prayer, fasting, and obedience. *Apostolic leaders know how to build a spirit of prayer into the life of the church (Matthew 21:13).*

HUSBANDRY

Uzziah also loved husbandry. Apostolic ministry thoroughly understands the spiritual pattern of farming:

plowing

sowing

watering

nurturing

pruning

reaping

There has been a great deal of teaching on sowing and reaping, but apostolic gifts

201

have the ability to attack the hardest of soils with an apostolic plow that breaks up any fallow ground (Hosea 10:12).

APOSTOLIC CHURCHES TRAIN UP WARRIORS AND TEACH THEM HOW TO USE THEIR SPIRITUAL WEAPONS, THE WORD, PRAISE, PRAYER, FASTING, DELIVERANCE, THE BLOOD, BINDING AND LOOSING, NETWORKING, TEAMWORK, ETC.

Apostles view their churches differently, and don't mind the times of pruning that occur (pruning is a common thing in apostolic churches). Where much is given, much is required and the Spirit of God will not tolerate any sin, rebellion, or dead wood laying around his apostolic forerunning church.

I have a mango tree in my yard that is beautiful. It has been growing for around ten years and is just a magnificent tree, casting wonderful shade. The problem is, however, it has never produced any fruit.

It has the appearance of health, and beauty, but is without any fruit.

Around the world, there are beautiful churches that remind me of that tree. They have multi-million dollar facilities, with grand steeples and are richly decorated with stained glass windows but, unfortunately, are bound in religion and bear no spiritual fruit. "And now also the ax is laid unto the root of the trees: therefore every tree which bringeth not forth good fruit is hewn down, and cast into the fire" (Matthew 3:10 KJV).

I have another mango tree that is nowhere near as large. It's not much to look at, and is really quite unattractive, however, when mango season comes, look out! It becomes so loaded down with fruit that the branches are in danger of breaking off. It bears so much fruit because it gets pruned every year. Pruning is required to bear fruit. Apostolic churches are pruned by the Holy Spirit and bear much fruit.

FIGHTING MEN

"Moreover Uzziah had an host of fighting men, that went out to war by bands, according to the number of their account by the hand of Jeiel the scribe and Maaseiah the ruler, under the hand of Hananiah, one of the king's captains. {12}

Governing Churches

The whole number of the chief of the fathers of the mighty men of valour were two thousand and six hundred. {13} And under their hand was an army, three hundred thousand and seven thousand and five hundred, that made war with mighty power, to help the king against the enemy" (2 Chronicles 26:11-13 KJV).

Uzziah had a host of fighting men. *Apostolic mantles attract spiritual warriors.* Apostolic ministry will...

> attract

> recruit

> gather

> train

> prepare the saints for spiritual battle

These warriors were not just to be looked at but were sent out into other territories to fight. Apostolic churches will raise up mighty warriors in these last days and send them forth into victorious battle. The word declares that they went forth and made war with mighty power to help their king. These are men empowered by God that understand that there is a great cause, reaching the world with the glorious gospel of Jesus Christ.

SPIRITUAL EQUIPMENT

"And Uzziah prepared for them throughout all the host shields, and spears, and helmets, and habergeons, and bows, and slings to cast stones" (2 Chronicles 26:14 KJV).

Uzziah raised up this great warrior host and equipped them. Apostolic churches train up warriors and teach them how to use their spiritual weapons, the word, praise, prayer, fasting, deliverance, the blood, binding and loosing, networking, teamwork, etc.

DIVINE STRATEGIES

"And he made in Jerusalem engines, invented by cunning men, to be on the towers and upon the bulwarks, to shoot arrows and great stones withal. And his name spread far abroad; for he was marvelously helped, till he was strong" (2 Chronicles 26:15 KJV).

Finally, we see Uzziah with inventions of warfare, a prophetic example of apostolic strategy. The 21st Century apostolic church will be a ministry of strategy. We've had two thousand years to get the gospel into the world and still our work is not yet accomplished. We need and will see divinely inspired apostolic strategies given by the Holy Spirit to enable us to reach the world with the gospel. Uzziah teaches us that God gave him strategies that helped him win in his generation. As the Scripture declares, "He was marvelously helped."

PRIDE AN APOSTOLIC PITFALL

"But when he was strong, his heart was lifted up to his destruction: for he transgressed against the LORD his God, and went into the temple of the LORD to burn incense upon the altar of incense" (2 Chronicles 26:16 KJV).

APOSTOLIC CHURCHES WILL RAISE UP MIGHTY WARRIORS IN THESE LAST DAYS AND SEND THEM FORTH INTO VICTORIOUS BATTLE.

It's sad to end this chapter with this verse, but God teaches us a great lesson here. The time is coming when the apostolic churches will finally punch through all the walls of demonic resistance that have tried to stop them. However, with these great victories will come a testing in that success. *Pride is one of the greatest weapons used against apostolic ministries.* Let us learn from Uzziah's example and not enter it.

In summary:

> "Humble yourselves therefore under the mighty hand of God, that he may exalt you in due time" (1 Peter 5:6 KJV).

Next we are going to discuss one of the most critical accusations against an apostolic church, that of being non-loving.

Governing Churches

☐ Character has nothing to do with reputation, which is what others think about you, but rather it is what God knows about you.

☐ The key to the success of apostolic ministry is the ability to continually put the Lord first.

☐ The word gift (*minchah*) is better translated as tribute. It is the regular payment of money made by one ruler or nation to another as acknowledgment of subjugation.

☐ Apostolic ministry gifts are not afraid of the prophetic and will build towers or platforms of ministry, providing a place for them to operate in their gifting.

☐ Apostolic leaders know how to build a spirit of prayer into the life of the church.

☐ The Holy Spirit prunes apostolic churches so they can bear much fruit.

Uzziah The Reformer

☐ Apostolic ministry will attract, recruit, gather, train, and prepare the saints for spiritual battle.

☐ Apostolic churches train up warriors and teach them how to use their spiritual weapons, the word, praise, prayer, fasting, deliverance, the blood, binding and loosing, networking, teamwork, etc.

☐ Pride is one of the greatest weapons used against apostolic ministries.

Governing Churches

CHAPTER 13
LOVE AND THE APOSTOLIC CHURCH

Apostolic churches have repeatedly been accused of being non-loving when in reality they are the most loving people in the world.

Apostles and prophets are often accused of being non-loving. This is especially true in developing or emerging apostolic churches that are setting things in order (1 Chronicles 15:13). You may have heard someone make a comment like, "There is no love in that church." It's unfortunate that people make such broad sweeping statements that target so many people.

I have been accused of being non-loving and it is really grievous to me. I have dedicated my entire life to ministering to people who may or may not appreciate it. However, it's interesting to note that I seldom am accused of being non-loving unless I have brought correction to someone or have ministered on a topic that challenged a person to change. False

211

accusations usually come from people being challenged by the Holy Spirit to mature.

Instead of dealing with their own faults, they begin to lash out at others in an effort to divert attention from themselves.

FALSE ACCUSATIONS USUALLY COME FROM PEOPLE BEING CHALLENGED BY THE HOLY SPIRIT TO MATURE.

Sometimes accusations are from people coming in from another church who have their own ideas or opinions of how things should be done. These folks are usually shocked to find out that things in an apostolic church are being done quite differently. If they bring with them any type of religious facade, it will be blown to pieces by the unwavering directness of the apostles and prophets. Apostles and prophets are the two foundation and belief system gifts that cause people to take a closer look at themselves and then change or run.

If they don't change, then they accuse the leaders of being non-loving as they look for a more comfortable, user friendly church.

APOSTLES, UNLIKE OTHERS, VIEW THE CHURCH AS AN INSTRUMENT TO ADVANCE THE KINGDOM OF GOD AND NOT AS A PLAYGROUND, RETIREMENT, OR DAYCARE CENTER.

A true leader must dare to confront and bring correction, out of the right spirit, when necessary. They must be freed from the fear of man or public opinion. When correction is necessary it's always easier to say nothing, but true love is not like that. Paul was sometimes harsh in his dealings with people, even to the point of turning them over to Satan. Not something that I am recommending you to do.

"Of whom is Hymenaeus and Alexander; whom I have delivered unto Satan, that they may learn not to blaspheme" (1 Timothy 1:20 KJV).

"Alexander the coppersmith did me much evil: the Lord reward him according to his works" (2 Timothy 4:14 KJV).

Knowing Paul's character, I'm sure that he exhausted every effort to reach these men. No minister of God wants to see people lost. Apostles, unlike others, view the church as an instrument to advance the kingdom of God and not as a playground, retirement or daycare center.

Somehow, our society seems to think that preachers are supposed to just be nice, and that everyone should be accepted just as they are and should never be required to grow up and mature. Not so with the rotor-rooter ministry of apostles and prophets. They see salvation of the lost as the *beginning* of the work and not the end.

Scripture records that Peter too, moved by the Spirit of God, had some harsh words with a couple in the church. "Then Peter said unto her, How is it that ye have agreed together to tempt the Spirit of the Lord? behold, the feet of them which have buried thy husband are at the door, and shall carry thee out. {10} Then fell she down straightway at his feet, and yielded

Love And The Apostolic Church

up the ghost: and the young men came in, and found her dead, and, carrying her forth, buried her by her husband" (Acts 5:9-10 KJV).

They left the church, but not in the way they would have liked. I wonder how many people standing by thought they were mistreated?

Of course, this is the extreme, but many people fail to realize that the word of God also confronts...

the wolves
(Acts 20:29, 30)

the dogs
(Philippians 3:2)

the deceitful workers
(2 Corinthians 11:13)

the religious spirits
(Matthew 23)

True, loving leaders are not afraid to challenge, watch, strengthen, encourage, and bring stability to the body of Christ. Instead of attacking our leaders for their courage in making a righteous stand, we should give them honor and appreciate them.

"Let the elders that rule well be counted worthy of double honour, especially they who labour in the word and doctrine" (1 Timothy 5:17 KJV).

Let's examine true love from an apostolic perspective and look at what love is and what love is not.

LOVE MISCONCEPTIONS

Apostolic churches have repeatedly and unfairly been accused of being unloving when in reality they are the most loving people in the world. One needs only to stop and ponder the accusations to discover that there is a misconception of what love really is. Some people who accuse an Antioch type of church of being unloving have been challenged to grow up, mature and advance. Others may have been prevented from doing something goofy when they thought the Spirit was leading them.

Many religious and unstable people think that unconditional love in the local church gives them license to do whatever "ministry" they want without any accountability. It also means that they can grow at their own speed and should never have any demands put on them. When challenged in a truly apostolic church,

Love And The Apostolic Church

they often retaliate by asking where the
love is. Then, they demand an
unconditional love, meaning that anything
goes, with no correction please. Many live
lives of sin and rebellion, insisting that the
church leaders cover it with soulish love
even if there is no repentance. However,
the truth is that love covers repentant
people and not rebellion.

We forget that God, who himself is love,
has written in his word some 1595 times
and in 1420 verses the word 'if'. Many are
trying to take that word out of the
expression of love in apostolic churches.
They use 1 Corinthians 13, the love
chapter, in their attempt to prove what
love is. Let's take a closer look at that
scripture.

"Though I speak with the tongues
of men and of angels, and have not
charity, I am become as sounding
brass, or a tinkling cymbal. {2} And
though I have the gift of prophecy,
and understand all mysteries, and
all knowledge; and though I have
all faith, so that I could remove
mountains, and have not charity, I
am nothing. {3} And though I
bestow all my goods to feed the
poor, and though I give my body to
be burned, and have not charity, it
profiteth me nothing. {4} Charity

217

suffereth long, and is kind; charity envieth not; charity vaunteth not itself, is not puffed up, {5} Doth not behave itself unseemly, seeketh not her own, is not easily provoked, thinketh no evil; {6} Rejoiceth not in iniquity, but rejoiceth in the truth; {7} Beareth all things, believeth all things, hopeth all things, endureth all things. {8} Charity never faileth: but whether there be prophecies, they shall fail; whether there be tongues, they shall cease; whether there be knowledge, it shall vanish away" (1 Corinthians 13:1-8 KJV).

EIGHT THINGS THAT LOVE IS

1. Long-suffering (*makrothumeo*)

Long-suffering is from the Greek word *makrothumeo*, and means that love will persevere patiently and bravely while enduring misfortunes and troubles. This long-suffering spirit is the manifestation of a love that does not lose heart during tough or hard times. It will also be long-spirited and patiently bear the offenses and false accusations of others. Notice that this is the first quality of love and in fact hardship is the first challenge

Love And The Apostolic Church

of any apostolic ministry. If there is any ministry gift that understands hardship it is the apostolic.

2. Kind *(chresteuomai)*

This is the only place in the New Testament where this word is used. Apostolic love is sympathetic, gentle, and cordial. Apostolic churches are filled with the kindest people that you have ever met. Kindness, however, doesn't mean that they are weak, meek, pious, or only soft spoken. This is not kindness from a religious perspective. It carries a sincere compassion for others yet commands maturity and resists flakiness.

3. Thinketh No Evil

Apostolic love is not motivated by evil thinking and apostolic people minister on divine things out of a pure conscience. One thing that they understand is that God tries the reigns of the heart. Motives are very important in the lives of apostolic people. Remember that apostles and prophets are foundation gifts, therefore they deal with belief systems, including the weighing out of their own motivation.

4. Rejoiceth In The Truth

Apostolic love longs to rejoice in truth. This is directly opposite of religious spirits who will only rejoice with you if they benefit from whatever has happened to you.

5. Beareth All Things

This is the Greek word *stego,* which means to cover, to hide by covering, or to ward off by covering. It is taken from the root word *stege* meaning to strengthen. Spiritual strength and fortitude are the most common traits of apostolic people. Strength to carry their own cross first and bear the burdens and hardships of ministry is definitely a sign of apostolic love. Apostolic people prepare others to carry their own crosses by imparting truth to them. Yes, they will certainly pray for the people, but they will not do their praying for them. Apostles are coaches and coaches will not run laps for the players.

6. Believeth

Antioch churches are faith-filled, believing churches. They carry an apostolic love that is unlike that of the world who are always suspicious of people. Moreover the apostolic church is eager to believe what a person says and will initially take them at their word. However, that does not mean that they are gullible, naive, or will believe just anything. They know how to judge with a righteous judgment, by the Spirit of God.

Love And The Apostolic Church

"Beloved, believe not every spirit, but try the spirits whether they are of God: because many false prophets are gone out into the world" (1 John 4:1 KJV).

7. **Hopeth** *(Elpizo)*

Elpizo means to expect and trust. The best meaning in the apostolic type of church is a refusal to take defeat as the final answer. Apostolic people have a pioneering grit that continues to propel them forward during great times of hardship, always looking toward the future with an enduring hope.

8. **Endureth** (*hupomeno*)

Hupomeno means to stay under, remain, to bear, have fortitude, and to abide. In short, *hupomeno* is a love that will never break rank. This apostolic *agape* is likened to a soldier who in the heat of battle has a steadfastness of purpose, will not abandon, and has an active positive fortitude that endures to the victorious end.

"Thou therefore endure hardness, as a good soldier of Jesus Christ. {4} No man that warreth entangleth himself with the affairs of this life; that he may please him who hath chosen him to be a soldier" (2 Timothy 2:3-4 KJV).

EIGHT THINGS THAT LOVE IS NOT

1. Apostolic Love Envieth (*zello*) Not

This means to possess ill will over another's advantages, or possessions, to desire something that belongs to another. Apostolic love does not envy or desire what belongs to another. On the contrary, the very nature of Antioch apostolic churches is to empower, impart, build, strengthen, and equip the saints for the work of ministry.

The word envy (*zello*) can also mean to busy one's self about another in the sense of an attempting to control them. Apostolic churches are never controlling nor manipulating. *Zello* also means to be strongly jealous.

2. Love Vaunteth Not

This is taken from the Greek word *perpereuomai,* which means to brag or to boast about ones' accomplishments in an excessive way. It also means to step on, or put down others in an effort to lift up one's self. Apostolic churches are teamwork ministries and they understand the value and importance of each other.

Love And The Apostolic Church

3. Not Puffed Up *(phusioo)*

This deals with pride. True love recognizes that any victories or accomplishments are made by hard work along with the blessings and grace of God. I once spoke with a man who could only talk about himself and his seemly great accomplishments. He spoke of how many nations he had been in as if he were putting notches on the wooden grips of a pistol. He was very much puffed up over himself. I have no desire to see him again.

> "Then he answered and spake unto me, saying, This is the word of the LORD unto Zerubbabel, saying, Not by might, nor by power, but by my spirit, saith the LORD of hosts" (Zechariah 4:6 KJV).

4. In Behavior Not Unseemly *(aschemoneo)*

To be unseemly is to be improper or indecent. One of the foundational principles of apostolic ministry is a righteous lifestyle and concern with holiness.

> "And they shall teach my people the difference between the holy and profane, and cause them to discern

between the unclean and the clean" (Ezekiel 44:23 KJV).

"Blessed are the pure in heart: for they shall see God." (Matthew 5:8 KJV)

5. Seeketh Not Her Own

Apostolic love is not self-centered. A striking character of apostolic churches is their concern for building and strengthening local churches worldwide. They are not trying to build their own kingdoms.

6. Not Easily Provoked *(paroyuno)*

Apostolic love cannot be easily exasperated to anger. There is a place for anger, but it is a passionate opposition to evil (Ephesians 4:26) and has nothing to do with soulish emotion.

"And when he had looked round about on them with anger, being grieved for the hardness of their hearts, he saith unto the man, Stretch forth thine hand. And he stretched it out: and his hand was restored whole as the other" (Mark 3:5 KJV).

"He that is slow to anger is better than the mighty; and he that ruleth his spirit than he that taketh a city" (Proverbs 16:32 KJV).

"Be ye angry, and sin not: let not the sun go down upon your wrath" (Ephesians 4:26 KJV).

7. Thinketh No Evil

Thinketh no evil is from the Greek word *logizomai,* which means to keep a written record of wrongs. This would denote one who remembers those sinful things about a person's past even though Jesus himself has forgiven them. An apostolic church is full of people who have sinned and fallen short of the glory of God.

8. Rejoiceth Not In Iniquity

Apostolic love takes no pleasure in evil of any kind, nor the misfortunes of others. Apostolic love does not rejoice or be glad in unrighteousness and injustice.

Love's goal -- to never fail!

LOVE AS A FATHER

Now, hopefully, a different perspective of the word love has been brought forth. Apostolic love is not a religious, soulish, mushy, or unrealistic approach to ministering to someone.

Governing Churches

True apostolic churches are fathering churches that love those in their care just like a father and mother who love their own children. We will never see the manifestation of the sons of God until we have spiritual fathers. A father's love has the children's best interest at heart even though the children may not be able to see it at the time.

I love my children unconditionally. No matter what they do, they are still my children and I will always love them unconditionally. But my unconditional love includes the responsibility to raise and nurture them in the admonition of the Lord. Therefore, to be a responsible father and a loving parent, I must help them mature and become responsible. I must continually point them to Jesus who is the author and finisher of their faith.

The same is true in the apostolic church. So next time someone asks the question, "Where is the love in that church?" we must take a moment to examine their definition of love.

APOSTLES LOVE SHEEP!

"As many as I love, I rebuke and chasten" (Revelation 3:19).

"But when we are judged, we are chastened of the Lord, that we

226

should not be condemned with the world" (1 Corinthians 11:32).

"My son, despise not the chastening of the LORD; neither be weary of his correction: {12} For whom the LORD loveth he correcteth; even as a father the son in whom he delighteth" (Proverbs 3:11-12).

If we have the love of God in our hearts and it projects through our lives, we will receive God's correction in these last days.

In the ensuing chapter we will look at one of the most serious problems in the restoration of the apostolic church; false apostles and how to identify them.

Governing Churches

☐ Apostles and prophets are often accused of being non-loving. This is especially true in developing or emerging apostolic churches that are setting things in order (1 Chronicles 15:13).

☐ Accusations usually come from people being challenged by the Holy Spirit to mature. Instead of dealing with their own faults, they begin to lash out at others in an effort to divert attention from them.

☐ Apostles and prophets are the two foundation and belief system gifts that cause people to take a closer look at themselves and then change or run.

☐ Apostles, unlike others view the church as an instrument to advance the kingdom of God and not as a playground, retirement or daycare center.

☐ The word of God confronts the wolves (Acts 20:29, 30), the dogs (Philippians 3:2), the deceitful

Love And The Apostolic Church

workers (2 Corinthians 11:13), and the religious spirits (Matthew 23).

☐ There are eight things that love is and eight things that love is not.

Governing Churches

CHAPTER 14
RECOGNIZING FALSE APOSTLES

False apostles "have the look." They stay abreast of the current religious fashions, dress, look, sayings, buzzwords, lingo, terminology, etc.

There will be at least three great opponents to the restoration of a fully operational apostolic church. They will be...

the spirit of Jezebel

the religious spirit

false apostles

Apostolic churches are equipped to handle Jezebel and the hypocrisy of religion, but false apostles and prophets will bring suspicion and reproach on those that are true. The word of God gives us several examples of the false and fallen such as Judas Iscariot, Balaam, and Diotrephes. Satan himself is the master counterfeiter and it is vital that the body of Christ be able to distinguish the true from the false. By God's grace we have the ability to see.

CAREFUL EXAMINATION

Many people are reluctant to closely examine the lives of their leaders for fear of being accused of being judgmental. We are not called to judge someone's salvation but rather to examine the fruit of one's character.

IF SATAN CAN
TRANSFORM HIMSELF
AND PRESENT A
DECEIVING IMAGE THEN
SO CAN A FALSE APOSTLE.

One way to help stay on course is to quickly discern the true apostolic from the false. Jesus said to the church of Ephesus, "I know thy works, and thy labour, and thy patience, and how thou canst not bear them which are evil: and thou hast tried them which say they are apostles, and are not, and hast found them liars" (Revelation 2:2 KJV).

The Ephesian church "tried" (Greek *peirazo*) those who said they were apostles. Evidently, there was a rise of false leaders who labeled themselves apostles that were coming into contact with the church at Ephesus. John commended the church for their ability to discern the genuineness of those who desired to labor among them.

The word tried *(peirazo)* means to prove one's character and steadfastness of faith. Here we see the approval of God in our putting one's character and steadfastness of faith to the test. Hirelings and false apostles will run, forsaking the sheep, when there is a battle or a hardship that affects them personally. Paul said, "For I know this, that after my departing shall grievous wolves enter in among you, not sparing the flock" (Acts 20:29 KJV).

The word encourages us by saying, "Beloved, believe not every spirit, but try the spirits whether they are of God: because many *false prophets* are gone out into the world" (1 John 4:1 KJV Italics added).

Here the word try is the Greek word *dokimazo,* which means to recognize as genuine after a careful examination.

There are three basic defenses in identifying and avoiding false apostles:

1. Know the characteristics and operations of a true apostle.

2. Become a solid student of God's word.

3. Submit to the counsel and protection of your "set man."

The grace of God and the witness of the Holy Spirit are necessary to assist us in discerning a false worker. Remember, Judas deceived even the Apostles of the Lamb. Whether he was a false apostle or a fallen apostle, he still managed to deceive those who were trained by our Lord himself. Thank God for the Holy Spirit!

We must not become associated with false apostles even for the sake of unity. I have turned down many preaching invitations because I would not be a participant on such platforms, even when those present could have been blessed. The word says, "Be ye not unequally yoked together with unbelievers: for what fellowship hath righteousness with unrighteousness? and what communion hath light with darkness?" (2 Corinthians 6:14 KJV). How much more so to be unequally yoked on a ministry platform.

I am often asked about the people who attend those meetings. My heart goes out to them, but they must get themselves out. I believe that the Holy Spirit reveals the false to people that are truly after God's own heart, but if they don't respond by leaving, then they are in great danger of the same deception coming over them.

Outlined below are 22 signs of a false apostle. Understanding these characteristics will not only help us identify a false apostle, but will also assist us in avoiding them as they appear.

22 SIGNS
OF A FALSE APOSTLE

1. Merchandisers

One of the most common signs of a false apostle is merchandising. A merchandiser is one who uses the ministry as a ruse or platform to sell products with the intent to make money. Ministry is a calling, it's work but not a job. False apostles use gimmicks, tricks, and clever what-evers to promote, manipulate and deceive. This would be your classic "snake oil, cure all" scenario.

These false merchandisers sell many gimmick items, including:

miracle water

sawdust from campmeeting floors

pieces of cut up revival tents for prayer clothes

rose peddles

prophet's healing juice from some
exotic root

bars of soap to wash away
witchcraft

the pitiful list goes on and on

I saw a "minister" hold up four white
letter envelops. He told the crowd that God
prophetically revealed to him that there
were four people there that needed healing
in their bodies. He went on to say that, the
first four people who came to the altar
with a one hundred dollar seed faith
offering would get their healing. That was
flagrant merchandising and a disgrace to
the gospel of Jesus Christ. I absolutely
believe in divine healing, but not for
money!

I support the distribution of ministry
resources and training materials like
books and tapes, provided they are offered
in good taste and in an appropriate
fashion.

Quality materials help the body of
Christ grow. It's important to study the
word and keep abreast of what the Spirit
of God is saying to the churches. Great
teaching resources are often unavailable

to us at other times. Much of our best teaching materials are what I call "black market resources" because they are seldom available at your local Christian bookstore. Especially if that Christian bookstore owner has a religious spirit.

FALSE APOSTLES USE GIMMICKS, TRICKS, AND CLEVER WHAT-EVERS TO PROMOTE, MANIPULATE AND DECEIVE.

False apostles are merchandisers and use various forms of gimmicks, products, prophecies, or prayers, to get money. If you find yourself in such a meeting, leave!

> "Then the LORD said unto me, The prophets prophesy lies in my name: I sent them not, neither have I commanded them, neither spake unto them: they prophesy unto you a false vision and divination, and a thing of nought, and the deceit of their heart" (Jeremiah 14:14 KJV).

2. Deceitful Workers

> "But what I do, that I will do, that I may cut off occasion from them which desire occasion; that wherein they glory, they may be found even as we. {13} For such are *false apostles,* deceitful workers, transforming themselves into the apostles of Christ. {14} And no marvel; for Satan himself is transformed into an angel of light. {15} Therefore it is no great thing if his ministers also be transformed as the ministers of righteousness; whose end shall be according to their works" (2 Corinthians 11:12-15 KJV Italics added).

Here, too, we see the mention of false apostles *pseudapostolos.* This is the only scripture with such a reference and these false apostles are called deceitful workers. A deceitful worker is one who has a tendency to lie or cheat with intent to deceive. A false apostle will represent or present something as being true when he knows that it is false. False apostles have dishonest acts designed to...

enslave

mislead

betray

False apostles offer deliberate misrepresentation of the facts with sophisticated, charming, flattering words or actions. Their motive is to pursue their own means using a cloak of deception, lies, and half truths thereby causing people to follow a wrong course of action.

3. Polished Showmen

> "... *transforming themselves into the apostles of Christ*" (2 Corinthians 11:14 KJV Italics added).

False apostles "have the look." They stay abreast of the current religious fashions, dress, look, sayings, buzzwords, lingo, terminology, etc. The Spirit of God has not transformed them, they have transformed themselves with carnal effort and marketing, becoming polished showman with false personalities. This is image without substance, personality without character, soulish flattery and carnal charm originating from the soul of man. "And no marvel; for Satan himself is transformed into an angel of light. {15} Therefore it is no great thing if his ministers also be transformed as the ministers of righteousness; whose end shall be according to their works" (2 Corinthians 11:14-15 KJV). If Satan can transform himself and present a deceiving image then so can a false apostle.

Jesus said, "Follow me, and *I will make* you a fisher of men" (Matt 4:19). Jesus does the making, there are no self-made Christians in the Lord's service, all are Christ made. False apostles use marketing techniques to mold their image and their stage presence. Avoid them at all cost! The person you see on the platform and behind the pulpit should be the very same person you see in person.

> "Let no man deceive you with vain words: for because of these things cometh the wrath of God upon the children of disobedience" (Ephesians 5:6 KJV).

> "Beware lest anyone cheat you through philosophy and empty deceit, according to the tradition of men, according to the basic principles of the world, and not according to Christ" (Colossians 2:8 NKJV).

4. Manifest False Moves Of The Holy Spirit, Especially Through False Prophecy

Recognizing False Apostles

In these last days, there are many who will say Jesus is the Christ and who will have what may appear to be moves of the Spirit but are not. A false prophet can counterfeit prophetic utterances. He can come across with a false authority and a false anointing, but he cannot give life to dry bones. We must learn to know people by the spirit and not fall into deception.

> Jesus told us, "take heed lest any man deceive you: {6} For many shall come in my name, saying, I am Christ; and shall deceive many" (Mark 13:5-6 KJV). And again he says, "Many will say to me in that day, Lord, Lord, have we not prophesied in thy name? and in thy name have cast out devils? and in thy name done many wonderful works? {23} And then will I profess unto them, I never knew you: depart from me, ye that work iniquity" (Matthew 7:22-23 KJV).

5. Beguiling (Tricks, Angles, Games and Secrecy)

> "For our exhortation was not of deceit, nor of uncleanness, nor in guile" (1 Thessalonians 2:3 KJV).

Governing Churches

To beguile implies the use of wiles while at the same time enticing others.

A wile is...

a sly trick

angle

game

scheme

double-talk

a calculation designed to deceive

False apostles are slick! Many false apostles look for photo opportunities with large crowds, making it appear that they have a large following. They do this with the intent of giving themselves credibility and the appearance of something they are not. They also try to maintain a mysterious air of secrecy about themselves. Behavior that is not normal, civil, or appropriate is an indication that something is wrong. Judas the traitor himself used secrecy as he, "sought means to betray him unto them *in the absence of the multitude*" (Luke 22:6 italics added).

6. Hang Out With Each Other

There is an old proverb, "birds of a feather flock together." Many false apostles use each other's ministries to lend credibility to one another. They often swap pulpits while merchandising one another's congregation. Beware of a team of false apostles.

ONE OF THE MOST COMMON SIGNS OF A FALSE APOSTLE IS MERCHANDISING.

---

7. Attach Themselves To True Apostles

Successful ministries often attract into their midst the false. Simon the sorcerer is a good example of someone that tried to attach himself to a true ministry for his own financial gain (see Acts Chapter Eight). These are often identified as the "name droppers." They seem to know everybody and in reality their connections are fabricated.

8. Liars

"... and thou hast tried them which say they are apostles, and are not, and hast found them *liars*" (Revelation 2:2 KJV Italics added).

Jesus gave us the first dark quality of a false apostle; one who is a liar. If anyone should be upright in their word, it's a Christian. The word says to let your yes be yes and your no be no (Matthew 5:37). Satan himself is the father of all liars as it is written, "Ye are of your father the devil, and the lusts of your father ye will do. He was a murderer from the beginning, and abode not in the truth, because there is no truth in him. When he speaketh a lie, he speaketh of his own: for he is a liar, and the father of it" (John 8:44 KJV).

FALSE APOSTLES MAY SPEAK ABOUT THE EVILS OF SIN, BUT THEY WILL NOT UPROOT IT IN THEIR OWN MIDST WHEN IT'S IN THEIR POWER TO DO SO.

9. Pushy

False apostles are driven and not led. They will do whatever they can to push open a door to have an opportunity to minister because they are power hungry. They use all the tricks in the book to get on ministry platforms in an attempt to advance their visibility. I can only imagine what it's like to screen people for highly visible ministries like TBN or the 700 Club. True apostles don't need to push themselves on others. They understand the scripture that declares, "A man's gift maketh room for him, and bringeth him before great men" (Proverbs 18:16 KJV). A pushy, demanding, driven person should cause one to put up a yellow flag of caution. Ministry is not about holding a single meeting, but is about the building of relationships between leaders, churches and people.

10. Self-Centered

False apostles only build relationships with people they perceive will advance their ministries, and have no time for the "little guy."

Years ago, I was with my wife at a conference dinner in another country. We had a wonderful time and were sitting at a table fellowshipping with some very friendly saints who we had just met. A man approached me saying that he was an evangelist and was interested in coming to the United States to preach in our church. I did take a few minutes to talk with him, but something happened, he asked me how many members we had in our church. When I told him that we had just started the church and it was very small he made a mad dash to the next "divine connection." This poor fellow had a very pitiful understanding of ministry. I never saw him again.

Other self-centered ministers have even gone so far as to try and steal my staff members because they felt that their ministry was far more important. This is totally a worldly and non-Christ like way to build a staff.

11. Seldom Address Sin

False apostles may speak about the evils of sin, but they will not uproot it in their own midst when it's in their power to do so. They may address sin, over there, or out there, but not when it's happening in their own lives or ministries. Some of these false apostles have a seducing, sexual charm about them that is totally inappropriate and should be offensive when encountered. False apostles always have some sort of hidden sexual sin in their lives. "For of this sort are they which creep into houses, and lead captive silly women laden with sins, led away with divers lusts" (2 Timothy 3:6 KJV).

False apostles will not turn God's people away from sin, "I have not sent these prophets, yet they ran: I have not spoken to them, yet they prophesied. {22} But if they had stood in my counsel, and had caused my people to hear my words, then they should have turned them from their evil way, and from the evil of their doings" (Jeremiah 23:21-22 KJV).

False apostles will not draw the line on sin. They will muddy the waters and not strike the line on issues of morality. True apostles and prophets, "shall teach my people the difference between the holy and profane, and cause them to discern between the unclean and the clean" (Ezekiel 44:23 KJV).

> "Follow peace with all men, *and* holiness, without which no man shall see the Lord" (Hebrews 12:14 KJV).

12. Will Not Correct

True apostles have a fathering spirit and they correct their spiritual children. False apostles seldom bring forth any correction nor will they raise up any sons.

Governing Churches

They shrink from the risk of offending anyone because they want to keep the sanctuary seats full at any cost.

13. Building Their Own Kingdoms

False apostles use their ministry for financial gain while supporting a lavish lifestyle. They often use high pressure offerings to manipulate people to finance their own kingdom. Love of money is the thread that weaves its way throughout the life and ministry of a false apostle (Matthew 6:33).

14. Loveth To Have The Preeminence

"I wrote unto the church: but Diotrephes, *who loveth to have the preeminence* among them, receiveth us not. {10} Wherefore, if I come, I will remember his deeds which he doeth, prating against us with malicious words: and not content therewith, neither doth he himself receive the brethren, and forbiddeth them that would, and casteth them out of the church" (3 John 1:9-10 KJV Italics added).

Although the word preeminence is closely related to being pushy, it's an overbearing desire to be first or above others. It's all about them, them, them. Jesus said, "So the last shall be first, and the first last ..." (Matthew 20:16 KJV).

Diotrephes, if not an apostle, was a leader in this church, but John The Beloved, singled him out as one who "loveth the presidency" or chief place and magnified himself in that office. The word states, "Let nothing be done through strife or vainglory; but in lowliness of mind let each esteem others better than themselves" (Philippians 2:3 KJV).

15.) Receiveth Us Not

False apostles are not approachable or hospitable, nor will they receive true apostles into their midst.

16. Malicious

"...prating against us with malicious words" (3 John 1:10 KJV).

False apostles are notorious with their use of malicious (harmful) words against others. The United States has many false apostles who are building their ministries by maliciously attacking, criticizing, and verbally tearing down every minister that is Holy Ghost filled. False apostles always talk in a malicious way about others.

17. Never Content

"and not content therewith" (3 John 1:10 KJV).

A false apostle is never satisfied or happy with what he has. This is not to be mistaken with the fortitude and perseverance of a true apostle, but crosses the line into covetousness.

"Thou shalt not covet thy neighbor's house, thou shalt not covet thy neighbor's wife, nor his manservant, nor his maidservant, nor his ox, nor his ass, nor any thing that is thy neighbor's" (Exodus 20:17 KJV).

18. Isolated

"... neither doth he himself receive the brethren, and forbiddeth them that would, and casteth them out of the church" (3 John 1:10 KJV).

It is not normal for apostles to be isolated from other ministry gifts in the world. No ministry is an island unto itself. False apostles isolate themselves and those whom they are influencing, even going to the point of excommunicating those who resist being isolated. Beware of the minister that tries to cut off any other godly voice into your life.

19. Love of Money

False apostles have a love of money that corrupts them. Scripture declares, "For the love of money is the root of all evil: which while some coveted after, they have erred from the faith, and pierced themselves through with many sorrows" (1 Timothy 6:10 KJV).

Because of this love for money, they will cross the line into deception for the rewards of divination. "And the elders of Moab and the elders of Midian departed with the rewards of divination in their hand; and they came unto Balaam, and spake unto him the words of Balak" (Numbers 22:7 KJV).

20. Promotion and Honor

> "For I will promote thee unto very great honour, and I will do whatsoever thou sayest unto me: come therefore, I pray thee, curse me this people" (Numbers 22:17 KJV).

The prophet Balaam was enticed to sin with the promise of promotion and the honor of men. Today this great sin entices and pulls on false apostles to enter the arena of a pride that loves to be admired as a great somebody.

21. Controlling

True apostles are the great liberators of God, where false apostles will bind one up through control and manipulation. False apostles will lord themselves over people. They control people through false prophecy and offer people titles and positions in an effort to keep them. Control is when coercion (manipulation and deception) is used to get people to do something that they don't want to do -- that's witchcraft.

22. Betrayers

Judas Iscariot was chosen to be one of the twelve apostles of the Lamb. Though he was chosen, he betrayed our Lord and sold him out for thirty pieces of silver. The heart of such a man is completely evil. "Then one of the twelve, called Judas Iscariot, went unto the chief priests, {15} And said unto them, What will ye give me, and I will deliver him unto you? And they covenanted with him for thirty pieces of silver. {16} And from that time he *sought opportunity to betray him*" (Matthew 26:14-16 KJV italics added).

Judas was an apostle who walked with Jesus. He saw the feeding of the multitudes, the dead raised, and lepers cleansed. He heard glorious words of everlasting life. Yet, he is listed over and over again in the gospels and remembered throughout history as the one "who sought opportunity to betray him."

Judas, although numbered among the apostles, did not act in a heated moment of passion. He was very calculating and cunning as he betrayed the Lord. He even sank so low as to lead the Roman soldiers to where Jesus was (Acts 1:16). To advance their own selfish agendas, false apostles will betray their closest of friends as we see Judas perform the darkest of evil deeds.

In the next chapter we will examine the very important issue of spiritual fathers and the sons of God.

Governing Churches

☐ There will be at least three great opponents to the restoration of a fully operational apostolic church. They will be the spirit of Jezebel, religious spirits, and false apostles.

☐ The Ephesian church "tried" (Greek *peirazo*) those who said they were apostles. The word tried *(peirazo)* means to prove one's character and steadfastness of faith.

☐ If Satan can transform himself and present a deceiving image then so can a false apostle.

☐ A wile is a sly trick, angle, game, scheme, double-talk, or a calculation designed to deceive.

☐ False apostles are slick!

☐ One of the most common signs of a false apostle is merchandising. A merchandiser is one who uses the ministry as a ruse or platform to sell products with the intent to make money.

Recognizing False Apostles

☐ Ministry is not about holding a single meeting, but is about the building of relationships between leaders, churches, people, etc.

☐ True apostles are the great liberators of God, where false apostles will bind one up through control and manipulation.

Governing Churches

CHAPTER 15
SPIRITUAL FATHERS & THE SONS OF GOD

The restoration of apostles will also bring the heart of fathers. One cannot be an apostle who does not have the heart of a spiritual father. Paul had a vested interest in the success of his spiritual son Timothy.

I come from a generation of preachers who grew up in the ministry without the benefit of a spiritual father. Like thousands of others we've had to glean whatever information we could through books, tapes, videos, seminars, conferences and brief encounters with men of God as they were hurried off platforms and away from the people. Often I have wondered how much more effective I might have become if I'd have had someone take a personal interest in the call of God on my life.

The restoration of apostles will bring the heart of fathers. *One cannot be an apostle who does not have the heart of a spiritual father.* Paul had a vested interest in the success of his spiritual son Timothy. You

257

can hear the heart of the father when Paul says, "For though ye have ten thousand instructors in Christ, yet have ye not many fathers: for in Christ Jesus I have begotten you through the gospel" (1 Corinthians 4:15 KJV).

IT TAKES MORE TIME TO RAISE A SPIRITUAL SON THAN IT DOES TO CONVERT A SINNER.

With the restoration of the apostolic team of apostles and prophets has come the cry of the Spirit within the prophet to turn the hearts of the fathers (apostles) to the children (sons) and the children to the fathers. For decades, we have been missing the spirit of the father in our churches as well as in our society. Our society is a mirror of the spiritual condition of our nation and we see an incredible increase of single parent homes. We see men abandoning their positions, responsibilities, wives, and their children like never before. This is a reflection of the spiritual condition of our world as we note the same pattern of abandonment taking place in the ministry. Two important questions are:

1. Who was your spiritual father?

2. Did you even have one?

The most probable answer is: "I didn't have one."

In the past many truly called ministry gifts have not taken the time to raise up spiritual sons or daughters. Some of the most visible ministers today have not taken the time to develop any true father-son relationships whatsoever. Some have deliberately gone out of their way not to create any relationships, and have focused more on building their own ministries rather than raising up spiritual sons.

DEVELOPING RELATIONSHIPS

There are many reasons for this lack of creating relationships, including:

A lack of those who desire to be raised up by true spiritual fathers.

An increase of rebellion in the heart of God's children.

Governing Churches

Some true fathers, in an effort to raise up spiritual sons, have allowed their humanity to be seen, only to find out that the sons were not able to handle it.

Many want blessing only and not the voice of change or correction that comes from true apostolic fathers.

Therefore, the result for many of God's leaders has been to follow the path of least resistance by concentrating on their own work of winning converts and avoiding the aggravation involved in raising up spiritual sons. It takes more time to raise a spiritual son than it does to convert a sinner.

I know our mandate is to reach the lost. However, the goal of evangelism is discipleship.

CHANGING TIMES

The times are changing! We are hearing a "turning voice" from the prophets, and with that voice, a change of heart is coming, turning it from self-centeredness to truly helping to raise up others. There is great spiritual hunger in the hearts of the apostles to again turn their affections on raising up spiritual sons. There will also be a great desire for sons to seek out the fathering spirit of the apostles.

Spiritual Fathers & The Sons Of God

The word tells us that all of creation is waiting on the manifestation of the sons of God (Romans 8:19). But I submit that without apostolic fathers there can be no manifestation of sons. Apostolic fathers ...

can be trusted

give guidance

protect

direct

nurture

shape and mold

discipline

encourage

impart wisdom

instill purpose

give hope

COUNTING THE COST

On an airplane returning to the USA from Africa I asked God what it would take to reach our city. His sudden response was, "You can't reach a city without talking to it." He encouraged me to "count the cost" while understanding that when one begins to prophetically speak to a city "there will come great spiritual opposition." With this in mind, he reminded me of when Abram fought the four kings who had taken his nephew, Lot, captive. Abram called upon those who were born in his own house to fight with him in battle. Abram fought the kings with his own spiritual sons, because sons will not run during the times of battle (Genesis 14:14).

We are in a time of great change. As we continue our journey through this awesome millennium let's seriously take heed of the words of God's prophet, Malachi, "And he shall turn the heart of the fathers to the children and the heart of the children to their fathers, lest I come and smite the earth with a curse" (Malachi 4:6).

In the following chapter, we will learn that the apostolic church will make a way for the manifestation of the sons of God. Get ready for victory!

Spiritual Fathers & The Sons Of God

SUMMARY: SPIRITUAL FATHERS & THE SONS OF GOD

☐ The restoration of apostles will also bring the heart of fathers.

☐ One cannot be an apostle who does not have the heart of a spiritual father.

☐ Paul had a vested interest in the success of his spiritual son Timothy.

☐ It takes more time to raise a spiritual son than it does to convert a sinner.

☐ The goal of evangelism is discipleship.

☐ Abram called upon those who were born in his own house to fight with him in battle.

Governing Churches

CHAPTER 16
THE
COMING
SONS OF GOD

If John the Baptist was alive today he would be labeled as an extremist, a non-conformist and a radical.

I was on my way to meet with a group of intercessors in New England who had given themselves to prayer and intercession for their territory, when the Spirit of God put it into my heart to encourage them in their labor. It seemed that the most important thing was to let them know that their prayers were effective even though there wasn't much to see in the natural. They were, in fact, making a way for something great.

JOHN THE VOICE

All over the world, there are newly emerging apostolic congregations who feel like they are little more than a voice crying out in the wilderness. Some even feel like they have been in a spiritual wilderness for years. For those who feel that way, let me point you to the apostolic ministry of John the Baptist.

THE REFORMING MESSAGE IS NOT VERY WELL RECEIVED IN TODAY'S SOCIETY BECAUSE PEOPLE ARE TRYING TO GET OTHERS TO CARRY THEIR CROSSES FOR THEM.

John the Baptist was sent forth as a prophetic voice in the wilderness that the Holy Spirit used to make a way for the coming of the Lord. His ministry was the forerunner to something else and, of course, someone greater. John the Baptist was also being prepared to decrease so that Jesus would increase (John 3:30). John preached a strong, reforming message of repentance that was unpopular in his day and not very popular today either. The reforming message is not very well received in today's society because people are trying to get others to carry their crosses for them.

John was misunderstood and did not fit into the religious system of his day. He obviously was not one who would conform to the ways of the Pharisees and Sadducees, but was a man with an incredible passion to fulfill his divine call. I am sure that he made his detractors quite nervous.

John was rejected and despised by the religious leaders and was martyred when he opposed the spirit of Jezebel (who later received his head as her trophy, Mark 6:25). Though there was great danger in preaching the gospel with such boldness, John did not let fear stop him.

EVANGELISM IS THE APOSTOLIC CHURCHES' FIRST MANDATE.

If John the Baptist was alive today he would probably never be booked as the keynote speaker for mainstream Christian conferences, and it would be rare for anyone to invite him for any special guest television appearances. Why? Because he would not be safe enough and would certainly be labeled as an extremist, a non-conformist and a radical. Today John would be asked to teach on prosperity, positive confession, or personal prophecy.

Unfortunately, some of our greatest platforms of ministry are being turned into

267

nothing more than financial seminars. John the Baptist would not qualify as a candidate for these meetings. We believe in sowing and reaping, but John would probably be bucking the current gospel fads and would have preached about dying to one's self, repentance, turning from sin, decreasing, and sowing one's own life as a matter of first things first.

I also think that John would be obedient to preach the gospel in the entire world. It's amazing how easy it is to get off focus and to be distracted into other areas of ministry. The balance for ministry in the apostolic church is a continual focus and reminding of our first call to reach the lost with the gospel of Jesus Christ. *Evangelism is the apostolic churches' first mandate.*

I once had a discussion with a pastor and friend who asked why I put a mandate of evangelism on his church. He said that perhaps reaching the lost was a call for my church only and it was unfair to put that commission on his. I was stunned to think that anyone would forget that there is but one great commission; "GO!" Jesus boldly declared, "Go ye into all the world and preach the gospel." It's hard to believe that we could lose sight of that. No wonder instability and flakiness lies at our charismatic doorsteps. Thank God for the restoration of the apostles and prophets.

A PROPHETIC EXAMPLE

John the Baptist is a prophetic example of intercession to thousands of people around the world that God is using to lay a spiritual road for the coming of the glorious church and ultimately the Lord Himself. I personally believe that the restoration of prayer, intercession, and the prophetic mantle in the 80's was actually the necessary spiritual equipment needed to lay down a prayer path for something else. That "something else" will be the manifestation of the glorious church. Sometimes we forget that the scriptures declare, "that He might present to Himself a glorious church not having spot, or wrinkle, or any such thing; but that it should be holy and without blemish" (Ephesians 5:27).

A GLORIOUS CHURCH

Saints, our prayers are making a way for the manifestation of the glorious church and we need the coming forth of the apostolic ministry gifts. I am talking about the true apostolic gifts, not the false who *label themselves* as apostle, prophet, bishop, reverend, most high reverend, arch bishop, etc.

Governing Churches

We may not fully understand the significance of the apostolic restoration and may even have difficulty at times relating with apostles and prophets, but we do need them. These gifts will help to prepare the church for a structural change and a glorious future. God has a design and a purpose, "now unto the principalities and powers in heavenly places might be known by the church the manifold wisdom of God" (Ephesians 3:10). *Apostolic ministry restoration is the precursor to the glorious church.*

The glorious church is where everybody is manifesting, "Christ in us the hope of glory" that will impact this world. The glorious church will be filled with those who are no longer watching from afar, everyone will get involved in the work.

MANIFESTING SONS

The apostolic church is making a way for the manifestation of the sons of God. "Beloved, now are we the sons of God, and it doth not yet appear what we shall be: but we know that, when he shall appear, we shall be like him; for we shall see him as he is" (1 John 3:1-2).

The sons of God are those who will rise up with an anointing that has not been seen in the earth since the times of the 1st Century apostles. Imagine the body of

The Coming Sons Of God

Christ being filled with men and women who carry God's anointing to such a degree that they turn the world upside down with gospel power. The glorious apostolic church will be filled with mature sons of God who will rise out of the midst of the Laodicean lukewarmness.

The great minister of prayer E. M. Bounds said, "Our fathers took their tea piping hot; we take ours iced. God is all on fire, and his church, if it be like Him, must also be aflame..."

THE APOSTOLIC CHURCH WILL CHALLENGE GOLIATH.

With some even the term sons of God makes them uneasy. However, it simply means, "that (we) are no longer children tossed to and fro and carried about with every wind of doctrine, but speaking the truth in love may grow up into him in all things which is the head even Christ from whom the whole body fitly joined together and compacted by that which every joint supplieth according to the effectual working in the measure of every part maketh increase of the body unto the

271

edifying of itself in love" (Ephesians 4:14-16).

Moreover, the word declares that this world "waiteth for the manifestation of the sons of God" (Romans 8:19). Are you ready? I think you are!

It's time for the awakening of the new apostolic voice. But, where are the apostolic gifts? Where is the prophetic cry of the Spirit? There are things happening in our nation that should be causing a mighty voice of opposition to come forth. However, in many cases instead of challenging the Goliath's of our territories we are attempting to sign peace treaties. Beloved, things are about to change. The apostolic church will challenge Goliath.

LAODICEAN PROPHETS

Sadly, many of God's apostolic gifts have decided to take one of the following directions:

> 1. Following the way of Balaam, they choose to merchandise their gifting as they look for honor, prestige, profit and promotions.

> 2. Some follow the way of the religious spirit and sit in darkened caves called apartments. With computer keyboards connected to

the Internet, they criticize everything and everyone that is doing something with a prophetic sound in their delivery.

3. Promulgating a gospel of escapism, doom and gloom, they search through the scriptures looking for a way to get off this earth.

4. False prophesies, visions, and dreams of coming judgment from hurricanes, fires, earthquakes, tornadoes, etc. To their own discredit, they are continually proven wrong, thus undermining true prophetic unctions.

5. Some have played it safe by resorting to ministries of personal prophecy only. They are in danger of crossing the line from His will to their own will, and moving into charismatic witchcraft.

6. Nevertheless some are standing on the battlefield with a mighty shout, holding their positions and striking the ground with an apostolic fortitude.

Governing Churches

Few have stepped into their place of turning the hearts of the fathers to the children and the children to the fathers. Regardless, I see the manifestation of the apostolic church confronting the brazen heavens, speaking out as a mighty prophetic voice, declaring Jesus as the only solution to this world's problems. I see a new breed of those who will do everything necessary to build God's church, an army of unified sons who are not ashamed of the gospel of Jesus Christ.

In summary, I want to encourage you to continue on and to "grow not weary in well doing, knowing that in due season we shall reap if we faint not." Your prayers are making a way (Luke 1:17). We do win! Jesus will build his church and "the gates of hell shall not prevail!"

In the next chapter, we'll look at prosperity and evangelism from an apostolic point of view.

The Coming Sons Of God

SUMMARY: THE COMING SONS OF GOD

☐ Evangelism is the apostolic churches' first mandate.

☐ John the Baptist is a prophetic example of intercession to thousands of people around the world that God is using to lay a spiritual road for the coming of the glorious church and ultimately the Lord Himself.

☐ Apostolic ministry restoration is the precursor to the glorious church.

☐ The glorious apostolic church will be filled with mature sons of God who will rise out of the midst of the Laodicean lukewarmness.

☐ The apostolic church will challenge Goliath.

Governing Churches

C H A P T E R 17
EVANGELISM
AND THE
APOSTOLIC
RESTORATION

With all this teaching on prosperity, money-cometh, sowing and reaping, 30, 60, 100, and financial blessings, "Can we please use some of it to reach the nations with the saving gospel of Jesus Christ?" Evangelism, not just for the chosen few, but for all believers.

I am going to take a chance and actually make some 'unsafe to some,' commentary. When you write a book like this that is read by a diverse group of believers, it creates a stir when moving from historical events of yesterday into more current topics affecting us all.

As with many of you, world evangelism has been wrenching my heart for years. Please bear with me as I write about a touchy subject -- prosperity and evangelism.

Today, there is much teaching on...

277

prosperity

money-cometh

sowing and reaping

30, 60, and 100 fold financial blessings

However, I have a question: May we please use some of it to reach the nations with the saving gospel of Jesus Christ?"

I don't want to step on any toes here, but I do believe in the "go ye" and "as they went preaching everywhere" concept of ministry (Mark 16:15,20). Evangelism is not just for the chosen few, but for all believers as well. To me the advancement of the gospel *is* the work of the ministry that we all ascribe to and are being apostolically equipped for (Ephesians 4:12).

I am not opposed to the prosperity message as long as we stay balanced, keep our focus right, and don't allow it to become the only message of our ministries. Do you realize that only about one percent of a typical church's income is actually used to preach the gospel outside of the four walls of the local church? Is this because only 1% of our messages deal with evangelism?

This means that most of the tithes and offerings received are used for maintenance only purposes rather than for advancing the gospel to the world (Acts 1:8). This is another reason why we need the restoration of an apostolic church full of apostolic teams. Without it, it becomes too easy to slip into the rut of consumer-only Christianity where the entire focus is inward, culminating in an hour of power on Sunday morning.

EVANGELISM IS SPELLED -- SWEAT!

Because of financial pressure, it is easy to get trapped into a one-message gospel. Because I am a pastor, I understand the financial strains put on a local church. However, this means we have to use that much more apostolic fortitude in breaking out of the four walls of our local churches. All of us are guilty to some degree, but we can change.

I tuned in Christian television one day and program after program had something about Biblical prosperity as a primary topic. I understand the message, the concept, and even the Biblical soundness of the doctrine when presented properly, but enough is enough; let's get on with it.

Governing Churches

Let's not allow our ministry platforms to turn into nothing more than Christian financial seminars and fund raising events. If we do, then another 2000 years won't be enough time to reach the world with the gospel.

Many are praying for apostolic strategies to reach their territories for Jesus. I think one of the first strategies for effective ministry is to take a close look at the fields that are ready for harvest (Matthew 9:37-38). Look at both the surrounding territories and then go out into the nations. Questions to ask include:

Where is the harvest field?

Who are the laborers?

Who are the equipped ones?

Where do I find team players?

What are the existing laborers doing?

Do not get so busy preaching a prosperity-only message that the lost get forgotten? Don't get upset with me, I am just as guilty as anyone and I repent.

Please don't take this the wrong way we do need prosperity. Gospel ministry cost money to carry out, but let's take that prosperity out into the harvest fields of the earth. How much will it take? Each of us must look to the Holy Spirit for that answer. To be truly apostolic, means that we keep our focus on reaching the lost.

SPECIALIST MINISTRY

I was involved in a conversation with a group of pastors which astonished me. Someone mentioned that many people were getting goofy in their thinking about the purpose of the local church. I replied that we must keep evangelism at the forefront as our first high calling to keep our churches and ministries stable. If not we become inward focused which releases all sorts of deteriorating forces against our churches. Another pastor standing nearby told me that he felt his church was called into a specialist ministry rather than evangelism. This means that some are called to do one thing and others something else. That thinking of course released him from any responsibility of reaching the lost because he was a specialist in something else. I believe that some are better in certain areas than others, but let's go a little farther as this plays out.

Since then, I have heard other, similar statements from people. Recently a lady told me that evangelism (go ye) was not her calling, but rather she was called into the prophetic dance or something along those lines. Another man told me that he was called to teach Biblical prosperity to the Yuppies (almost an unbelievable statement indeed). Another told me that he wanted to pay for my airline ticket on one of our Global Cause apostolic trips but he himself was not called to go, nor has he ever gone to any nation. Others have told me that they are only called to certain cities etc. It is important to know that "go ye" does not mean "go" to only some evangelistic specialist.

From these statements, and many more like them, it's apparent that there is a major shift in thinking creeping into the church. Evangelism is no longer an agreed upon first purpose. When, in fact, evangelism is the first order of business for any believer, specialist, the church, and of course, the apostolic church.

God set in the church the five fold ministry gifts of apostles, prophets, evangelist, pastors, and teachers for the perfecting of the saints for the work of the ministry (comma deliberately deleted by me -- Ephesians 4:12).

> What is the work of the ministry?
> Even though it may have many
> facets to it, there must remain a

solid foundational purpose and that is evangelism.

What is evangelism?
Webster defines it as preaching the gospel. Evangelism is the reaching of the lost with the gospel of Jesus Christ using various strategies and methods.

APOSTOLIC CHURCHES ARE WORKING CHURCHES.

If evangelism does not remain at the forefront, then the church becomes...

self-centered

apathetic

program-driven

entertainment-oriented

lukewarm

backslidden

hidden behind a form of godliness

defending a powerless life

Governing Churches

The word declares, "He that is wise wins souls" (Proverbs 11:30). The Holy Ghost himself is wisdom and his wisdom will look first to the harvest fields (Matthew 9:37-38). Let wisdom have its place again in the church. Money, the anointing, power, dunamis etc. is for the work of ministry.

"Go ye," and tell everybody that Jesus Christ himself is resurrected from the grave and he is the only begotten Lamb of God that takes away the sin of the world. Jesus declared that if he was lifted up that he would draw all men unto himself (John 12:32). How will they know without a preacher (Romans 10:14)? Did he say preacher, or dancer? Nothing against dancers! But you understand. The first calling of a church's body of assembled called out ones is to witness.

It's time to go into the highways and byways and compel sinners to come in (Luke 14:23). The calling of the church is to be equipped for work. Apostolic churches are working churches. Evangelism is spelled -- sweat!

This whole thing is not about specializing in some sort of "my ministry syndrome" and forgetting our first calling.

I am reminded of a statement from Dr. Oswald J. Smith. "The supreme task of the Church is the evangelization of the world.

Evangelism & Apostolic Reformation

But note that it is the evangelization, not the Christianization of the world. It is the work of witnessing, spreading the Good News, telling the story; namely, giving every man, woman and child a fair chance to accept Christ. We cannot but proclaim the message to all, and He will gather in His own, for his sheep hear His voice and they follow Him" (John 10:3-4).

Why do we need to keep evangelism at the forefront? Two billion people have never heard the name of Jesus. Not even one time! Five and a half billion people are not born again. In Western Europe church attendance is decreasing by 7000 people per day. Belgium is less than 1% Christian and France less than 3%. We must pray, send, go.

What a great opportunity for the restoration of the apostolic church. Yes, there is a new apostolic reformation taking place. Why? Because it's harvest time!

Finally, there is a 19th Century militant song written by an unknown author of the daring of the early apostles who dedicated and risked their lives for the gospel's sake.

The Son of God Goes Forth to War

A glorious band, the chosen few
On whom the Spirit came,

Governing Churches

Twelve valiant saints, their hope they
knew,
And mocked the cross and flame,

They met the tyrant's brandished steel,
The lion's gory mane,

They bowed their necks, the death to feel:
Who follows in their train?

**It's time to join the new apostolic
reformation!**

SUMMARY: EVANGELISM
AND THE APOSTOLIC RESTORATION

☐ Only about one percent of a typical church's income is actually used to preach the gospel outside of the four walls of the local church.

☐ Because of financial pressure, it is easy to get trapped into a one-message gospel.

☐ It is important to know that "go ye" does not mean "go" to only some evangelistic specialist.

☐ Evangelism is no longer an agreed upon first purpose. When, it fact, evangelism is the first order of business for any believer, specialist, the church, and of course, the apostolic church.

☐ Money, the anointing, power, dunamis etc. is for the work of ministry.

☐ Evangelism is spelled -- sweat!

Governing Churches

Appendix

Top 48 Gateway Cities
and Territories
in the United States
according to population

US. Census Bureau estimates for July 1, 1998

Ranking	Territory	Population
1. New York, Northern New Jersey, Long Island		20,124,377
2. Los Angeles, Riverside, Orange County		15,781,273
3. Chicago, Gary, Kenosha		8,809,846
4. Washington, Baltimore		7,285,206
5. San Francisco, Oakland, San Jose		6,816,047
6. Philadelphia, Wilmington, Atlantic City		5,988,348
7. Boston, Worcester, Lawrence		5,633,060
8. Detroit, Ann Arbor, Flint		5,457,583
9. Dallas Fort Worth		4,802,463
10. Houston, Galveston, Brazoria		4,407,579
11. Atlanta		3,746,059
12. Miami, Fort Lauderdale		3,655,844
13. Seattle, Tacoma, Bremerton		3,424,361
14. Phoenix, Mesa		2,931,004
15. Cleveland, Akron		2,911,683

Appendix

16. Minneapolis, St. Paul	2,831,234
17. San Diego	2,780,592
18. St. Louis	2,563,801
19. Denver, Boulder, Greeley	2,365,345
20. Pittsburgh	2,346,153
21. Tampa, St. Petersburg, Clearwater	2,256,559
22. Portland, Salem	2,149,056
23. Cincinnati, Hamilton	1,948,264
24. Kansas City	1,737,025
25. Sacramento, Yolo	1,685,812
26. Milwaukee, Racine	1,645,924
27. Norfolk, Virginia Beach, Newport News	1,542,143
28. San Antonio	1,538,338
29. Indianapolis	1,519,194
30. Orlando	1,504,569
31. Columbus	1,469,604
32. Charlotte, Gastonia, Rock Hill	1,383,080
33. Las Vegas	1,321,546
34. New Orleans	1,309,445
35. Salt Lake City, Ogden	1,267,745
36. Greensboro, Winston Salem, High Point	1,167,629
37. Nashville	1,156,225
38. Buffalo, Niagara Falls	1,152,541
39. Hartford	1,143,859
40. Providence, Fall River, Warwick	1,122,974
41. Austin, San Marcos	1,105,909
42. Memphis	1,093,427

Governing Churches

43. Rochester	1,081,883
44. Raleigh, Durham, Chapel Hill	1,079,873
45. Jacksonville	1,044,684
46. Oklahoma City	1,038,999
47. Grand Rapids, Muskegon, Holland	1,037,933
48. West Palm Beach, Boca Raton	1,032,625

COME VISIT WITH US

Hello friends and partners!

In addition to preaching the gospel around the world, we also have a powerful local church in South Florida.

The Spirit of God told us to start a church and raise up people in strength and power who would reach their city and impact the world. SOLM has an international apostolic prophetic call, as well as a mandate to raise up a strong local church by ministering to the whole family.

SOLM has the reputation of being a place where you can receive what you need from the Lord; whether it be healing, miracles, deliverance, restoration, victory, or success. Why? Because with God all things are possible.

SOLM' uniqueness is being recognized and sought after as we continue growing in spiritual liberty, influence, strength and power.

We invite you to come and receive your miracle breakthrough and to be a part of what the Spirit of God is doing in this hour.

In the Master's service,

Jonas Clark

PROPHETIC OPERATIONS

The prophets may give personal prophecies, but their revelation gifting goes way beyond personal prophecy. Power, money, prestige, honor, promotion, and enticements, with smooth flattering sayings, are all demonic assignments designed to pull on any common ground that might be in the heart of God's prophetic ministers.

Our society is filled with those who come into our churches who have formerly opened themselves up to new age mysticism, witchcraft, the occult, and spiritualism. To protect the flock from false anointings and familiar spirits, there is a proper order in which the Holy Spirit likes to flow.

A spiritist is one who operates in the realm of the spirit without the Spirit himself. How do we tell the difference between spiritualism and true prophetic operations?

ISBN 1-886885-02-8
Softcover Price only $9.99

EXPOSING SPIRITUAL WITCHCRAFT

Spiritual witchcraft is the power of Satan. Its purpose is to control and manipulate you.

The weapons of witchcraft are emotional manipulation, spiritual and religious control, isolation, soul ties, fear, confusion, loss of personal identity, sickness, depression and prophetic divination.

Those caught in the snare of this spirit struggle all their Christian life to remain stable in their walk with Christ.

Topics include: the character of spiritual witchcraft, the weapons of witchcraft, the road to deception and lastly -- breaking free!

I fought this spirit from April to November and won. So can you!

ISBN 1-886885-00-1
Softcover Price only $9.99

JEZEBEL, SEDUCING GODDESS OF WAR

Jezebel is the warrior goddess who has gone unchallenged in our generation. Dr. Lester Sumrall said that she would be the greatest opposer of the apostolic church before the coming of the Lord. In 1933 Voice of Healing Prophet William Branham had a vision of her rising to take control.

Some people write about things that they know nothing about. Not this time! It is time to barbecue this spirit.

ISBN 1-886885-04-4
Softcover Price only $11.99

50 EARMARKS OF AN APOSTOLIC CHURCH

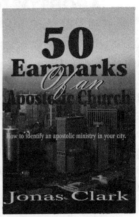

Jesus said, "I will build my church and the gates of hell shall not prevail." So what kind of church is it that Jesus is building? Is it a religious church? A traditional church? A defeated church? Or is it a glorious church without spot or wrinkle?

Right now we are experiencing an awesome paradigm shift in ministry. The Holy Spirit is moving us into a time of the restoration of the apostolic ministry. All over the world God is birthing apostolic churches. But what do they look like? What makes them so different? Is there one in your city? In this thought-provoking book Jonas teaches you 50 earmarks of an apostolic church in your city. It's time to cross the bridge into the apostolic. Are you ready to be a part of an exciting glorious church?

ISBN 1-886885-06-0
Softcover Price Only US$4.99

MOVING IN THE APOSTOLIC

Moving in the Apostolic is one of the most important teachings that Jonas has to offer the apostolic church. In it he gives us strong prophetic insight into the direction of the church. Jesus declared, "I shall build my church and the gates of hell  shall not prevail." Herein Jonas describes in distinct detail where the church is now and where she is going. For those of you who are apostolic and prophetic, this is a must have teaching series.

1.) Apostolic Positioning 2.) Purpose of the church, Pastoral or Apostolic? 3.) The Apostolic Dimension 4.) Gathering of the Sent Ones 5.) Positioned for Apostolic Release 6.) How to be an Apostolic Reformer

(6 tape classic cassette teaching series ..... Price only $30.00)

APOSTOLIC LIVING & TERRITORIAL CHURCHES

After traveling to many different cities around the world Jonas has discovered that territories differ spiritually. Many are trying to live in their city without discerning what principalities and powers are at work. In this revealing teaching series learn how to discern the spiritual climate over your city, what it is that buffets your ministry and how to make the "shift" necessary to live in victory.

1.) Living in Lukewarm Cities 2.) How to Live in Persecution 3.) Jezebel's Spiritual Climate 4.) Reformation Living During Opposition

(4 tape classic cassette teaching series ..... Price only $20.00)

THE
FIVE STAGES OF
THE APOSTOLIC
CHURCH

Are you ready to occupy the 21st century? This tape series contains a revelation that Jonas received after much prayer of the great changes coming to the church for this new millennium. In this dynamic teaching series learn how you will be challenged to move into a greater anointing and capacity of God's Spirit. You will learn about the five stages of apostolic authority including the territorial entrance, the pioneering stage, the building stage, the governing voice, and the spiritual hub. This is a "now word" to the church.

(3 tape classic cassette teaching series ..... Price only $15.00)

OTHER BOOKS BY JONAS CLARK

50 Earmarks of an Apostolic Church
ISBN1-886885-06-0

Exposing Spiritual Witchcraft
ISBN 1-886885-00-1

Jezebel, Seducing Goddess of War
ISBN 1-886885-04-4

Imaginations, Don't Live There!
ISBN 1-886885-03-6

Prophetic Operations
ISBN 1-886885-02-8

Religious Spirits
ISBN1-886885-01-X

Available in quality Christian
bookstores
or
on the Internet
http://catchlife.org

Spirit of Life Ministries
27 West Hallandale Beach Blvd.
Hallandale, Florida 33009
(954) 456-4420